A-LEVEL YEAR 2

STUDENT GUIDE

WJEC/Eduqas

Business

Business analysis and strategy

Mark Hage

Tracey Bell

HODDER
EDUCATION
AN HACHETTE UK COMPANY

Hodder Education, a Hachette UK company, Blenheim Court, George Street, Banbury, Oxfordshire OX16 5BH

Orders

Bookpoint Ltd, 130 Park Drive, Milton Park, Abingdon, Oxfordshire OX14 4SB

tel: 01235 827720

fax: 01235 400401

e-mail: education@bookpoint.co.uk

Lines are open 9.00 a.m.–5.00 p.m., Monday to Saturday, with a 24-hour message answering service. You can also order through the Hodder Education website: www.hoddereducation.co.uk

ISBN 978-1-5104-1936-0

First printed 2018

Impression number 5 4

Year 2022 2021

This Guide has been written specifically to support students preparing for the WJEC Eduqas and WJEC A-level Business examinations. The content has been neither approved nor endorsed by WJEC/Eduqas and remains the sole responsibility of the author.

Cover photograph: Sashkin/Shutterstock

Typeset by Integra Software Services Pvt. Ltd., Pondicherry, India

Printed in Dubai

Hachette UK's policy is to use papers that are natural, renewable and recyclable products and made from wood grown in sustainable forests. The logging and manufacturing processes are expected to conform to the environmental regulations of the country of origin.

Contents

■Getting the most from this book

Exam tips

Advice on key points in the text to help you learn and recall content, avoid pitfalls, and polish your exam technique in order to boost your grade.

Knowledge check

Rapid-fire questions throughout the Content Guidance section to check your understanding.

Knowledge check answers

1 Turn to the back of the book for the Knowledge check answers.

Summaries

■ Each core topic is rounded off by a bullet-list summary for quick-check reference of what you need to know.

Exam-style questions

Commentary on the questions

Tips on what you need to do to gain full marks, indicated by the icon **e**

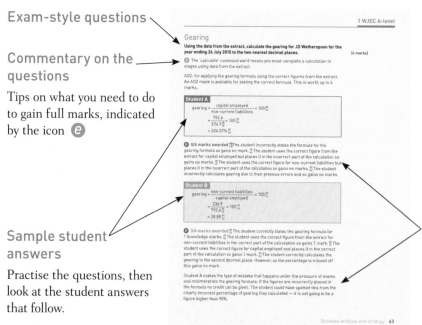

Commentary on sample student answers

Read the comments (preceded by the icon **e**) showing how many marks each answer would be awarded in the exam and exactly where marks are gained or lost.

Sample student answers

Practise the questions, then look at the student answers that follow.

■About this book

This guide has been written with one goal in mind: to provide you with the ideal resource for your revision of the second year of the WJEC Eduqas Business A-level.

In your study of the subject you will look at business in a variety of contexts, small and large, national and global, service and manufacturing. This book covers the theme of Unit 3/Component 2: Business analysis and strategy.

The **Content Guidance** section offers concise coverage, combining an overview of key terms and concepts with identification of opportunities for you to illustrate higher-level skills of analysis and evaluation.

The **Questions & Answers** section provides examples of stimulus materials and the various types of questions that you are likely to face: both structured and data-response questions. The questions cover both WJEC A-level and WJEC Eduqas A-level Business. They also give explanations of command words that can be applied to any question with the same word. The answers are also explained in detail, including the grades obtained.

A common problem for students and teachers is the lack of resources and in particular exam-style questions that cover individual areas of study. The questions in this guide are tailored so you can apply your learning while a topic is still fresh in your mind, either during the course itself or when you have revised a topic in preparation for the examination. Along with the sample answers this should provide you with a sound basis for sitting your exams in Business.

Pre-existing knowledge

You will already have completed the first year of your course so you will have covered a large body of business theory. Your existing business knowledge and skills will need to be developed through an interest in the current news in terms of businesses you are familiar with, such as Apple and McDonald's. Business is a subject that requires you to apply key terms to real businesses so an interest in businesses in the news will help you significantly to contextualise the theories. It is the really enjoyable part of the subject, and will assist you towards scoring highly in the exam.

Content Guidance

■ Data analysis

The process of **data analysis** transforms raw data into helpful information that can be used to analyse business situations. There are various methods, including:

- **Pie charts**, which are a type of graph in which a circle is divided into sectors to represent a proportion of the whole. The example in Figure 1 shows the total market for four products from which you may be asked to calculate and/or interpret the data, such as the market share of one product.
- **Histograms**, which consist of rectangles whose area is proportionate to how often a variable occurs in the set of data.
- **Index numbers**, which are a useful way of comparing information. An index number is a figure that shows a price or quantity compared with a starting point, known as the base value. The base value will normally start at 100. For example, Table 1 shows the costs of manufacturing in various countries compared to the USA, with the USA as the base value of 100. The Czech Republic's manufacturing costs were lower than the USA in 2004, but higher than the USA in 2014.

Table 1 Manufacturing costs in selected countries relative to the cost of manufacturing in the USA

Country	Indexed manufacturing costs 2004 (USA = 100)	Indexed manufacturing costs 2014 (USA = 100)
Czech Republic	96.6	106.7
Canada	104	115.4
Taiwan	92.3	97.2
UK	107.4	108.7
South Korea	98.7	102.4
India	112.7	111.5
Brazil	96.8	123.6

Source: The BCG Global Manufacturing Cost-Competiveness Index, www.bcgperspectives.com

Summary

After studying this topic, you should be able to:
- present, interpret and analyse data, including pie charts, histograms and index numbers

Data analysis
The process of transforming raw data into usable information, in order to present, interpret and analyse a business situation.

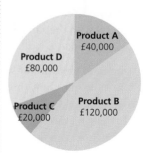

Figure 1 The sales of four products that make up the total market

Knowledge check 1

Give one reason why data analysis is important to a shop selling cakes.

■ Market analysis

The process of **market analysis** involves collecting information about the market the business is operating in, in order to create effective objectives to ensure success. This can include collecting information on the size of the market, the business's relative market share, the economic and political background to the market and then creating strategies.

Both quantitative and qualitative data can be used by a business to analyse its market and its customer needs currently and in the future:

- **Quantitative data** involve the use of numbers such as the size of the market, the growth of the market or the number of customers a business has, for example the number of 50-year-old men who have taken up cycling in the last 12 months.
- **Qualitative data** look at views and opinions, but do not provide statistically reliable information, for example asking cyclists how comfortable a new design of top is to wear.

Price elasticity of demand (PED)

It is important for a business to look at the amount of goods or services it has sold compared to the prices it charges. It can do this by calculating the **price elasticity of demand (PED)**. A formula is used in which the percentage change in quantity demanded is divided by the percentage change in price.

Example

A business is looking at reducing its price to its customers from £60 to £40. Sales are currently 15,000 but the demand curve in Figure 2 predicts sales will reach 25,000 if the price is reduced.

$$\text{PED} = \frac{\text{percentage change in quantity demanded}}{\text{percentage change in price}}$$

$$\text{Percentage change in quantity demanded} = \frac{(25,000 - 15,000 = 10,000)}{15,000}$$

$$= 0.66 \times 100 = 66\%$$

$$\text{Percentage change in price} = \frac{(£40 - £60 = -£20)}{£60}$$

$$= -0.33 \times 100 = -33\%$$

$$\text{PED} = \frac{66\%}{-33\%} = 2$$

Conclusion: this value means demand is sensitive to the price of the product. Demand is elastic, as predicted in Figure 2.

Exam tip

You must be able to calculate, analyse and evaluate the PED for a specific business context.

Market analysis The process of collecting information about the market the business is operating in, in order to create effective objectives to ensure success.

Price elasticity of demand (PED) Measures the responsiveness of demand after a change in price.

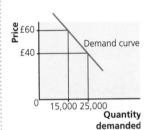

Figure 2 Price elasticity of demand calculation

Knowledge check 2

Define price elasticity of demand.

Interpreting price elasticity of demand

The values from price elasticity of demand calculations can give a business an indication of how sensitive, or elastic, its products are to changes in price. The values are:

- **If PED = 0 or less**. This means demand is perfectly inelastic. The demand for the product does not change at all when the price changes. This means the demand curve will be vertical.
- **If PED is between 0 and 1**. This means the percentage change in demand from the first to the second level of demand is smaller than the percentage change in price. Demand is inelastic.
- **If PED = 1**. This means the percentage change in demand is exactly the same as the percentage change in price — demand is unit elastic. The percentage rise in the price of the product would lead to exactly the same percentage fall in demand, leaving total spending on the product the same at each price level.
- **If PED = 1 or more**. This means demand is very sensitive to the price of the product — demand is elastic. A percentage rise in the product price would mean a more pronounced fall in the demand for the product. For example, if the price of the product went up 10%, the demand for the product would go down by 20%.

Evaluating the impact of price elasticity of demand on revenue

Factors include:

- **The number of close substitutes**. The closer substitutes there are in the market, the more elastic is demand as customers find it easier to switch to another product, potentially reducing revenue. The opposite effect occurs for goods that have few substitutes.
- **The cost of switching between products**. If there are costs involved in switching to another product, then demand is more likely to be inelastic, making revenue easier to achieve and maintain.
- **Whether the product is a luxury or essential to the customer**. Necessities tend to have an inelastic demand, making changes in revenue less volatile, but luxury products tend to have a more elastic demand, meaning changes in revenue can fluctuate significantly.

A business manufacturing products that are price elastic can try cutting its costs and lowering its prices to maintain revenue. Alternatively, it can attempt to make its products more price inelastic, for example through branding or marketing. Many businesses make smartphones but Apple smartphones are especially sought after and therefore Apple is able to charge higher prices and generate more revenue as its products are more price inelastic than those of other competitors.

Income elasticity of demand (YED)

Income elasticity can be used by a business to judge how it would be affected by economic change. It can do this by calculating the **income elasticity of demand (YED)**. A formula is used in which the percentage change in quantity demanded is divided by the percentage change in income.

Exam tip

Discuss the possible elasticity or inelasticity of demand to help you to answer an evaluative question.

Knowledge check 3

What is an advantage to a business of an inelastic good?

Exam tip

Try and identify the most relevant effects on elasticity in a case study.

Income elasticity of demand (YED) Measures the responsiveness of demand after a change in customer income.

Example

A consumer with an income of £20,000 buys 20 music downloads per year. Following an increase in their income to £40,000, this consumer now buys 40 music downloads per year (Figure 3).

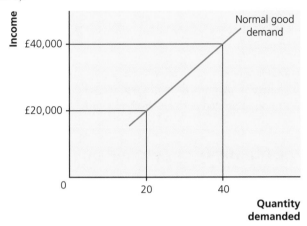

Figure 3 Income elasticity of demand calculation: normal goods

$$\text{YED} = \frac{\text{percentage change in quantity demanded}}{\text{percentage change in income}}$$

$$\text{Percentage change in quantity demanded} = \frac{(40 - 20 = 20)}{20} = 1 \times 100 = 100\%$$

$$\text{Percentage change in income} = \frac{(£40,000 - £20,000 = £20,000)}{£20,000} = 1 \times 100 = 100\%$$

$$\text{YED} = \frac{100\%}{100\%} = +1$$

Conclusion: this positive figure means that the good (music downloads) is a normal good. Because the answer is 1, demand for music downloads responds less than proportionately to a change in income. This means the good is not a necessity like food but is a relative luxury for the individual. Demand therefore is sensitive to the price of the product — demand is elastic.

Interpreting income elasticity of demand

- **Normal goods** have a positive income elasticity of demand. As a consumer income rises, more is demanded at each price so the product is income elastic, for example pasta or bread.
- **Normal necessities have a positive income elasticity of demand** of between 0 and +1. Demand is rising less than proportionately to a change in income.
- **Luxury goods and services have a positive income elasticity of demand** of more than +1. Demand rises more than proportionately to a change in income.
- **Inferior goods have a negative income elasticity of demand**, meaning that demand falls as income rises. For example, a consumer with an income of £40,000 buys 20 jars of value coffee per year. Following an increase in their income to £50,000, the consumer now buys 18 jars of value coffee per year (Figure 4).

Knowledge check 4

Define income elasticity of demand.

Normal goods These have a positive income elasticity of demand and there is a shift to the left in the demand curve. This means as incomes rise so does the demand at each price (e.g. clothing, household appliances).

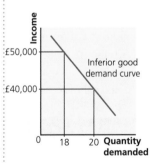

Figure 4 Income elasticity of demand calculation: inferior goods

$$\text{YED} = \frac{\text{percentage change in quantity demanded}}{\text{percentage change in income}}$$

Percentage change in quantity demanded $= \dfrac{(18 - 20 = -2)}{20} = -0.1 \times 100 = -10\%$

Percentage change in income $= \dfrac{(£50,000 - £40,000 = £10,000)}{£40,000} = 0.25 \times 100 = 25\%$

$\text{YED} = \dfrac{-10\%}{25\%} = -0.4$

This negative figure means that the good (value jars of coffee) is an inferior good — demand does not respond significantly to a change in income. Demand will reduce when incomes rise, as consumers will prefer to buy branded coffee, which is seen as more of a luxury.

Evaluating the impact of income elasticity of demand on revenue

Income elasticity of demand is important as it can help a business to decide how sensitive its products are in terms of demand when income changes. The more a business can charge a customer for its product without affecting the demand for it, the more potential profit it can make. Income can change due to:

- **Recession.** During a recession, incomes will reduce so consumers will become more price-sensitive to a business's products. For normal goods, demand will reduce as income is reducing. For inferior products, demand is likely to rise as the demand for luxury products falls due to the drop in income. For normal necessities, demand will fall but more slowly than the fall in income.
- **Taxation.** If the rate of **income tax** increases, becoming a higher percentage of income, then demand will fall for normal, luxury and normal necessities as stated above. The demand for inferior goods will rise as income falls, but proportionately more slowly. If the rate of income tax decreases, the opposite for each type of good will be the case.

If a product is sensitive to price, a business could:

- Focus the product on higher-income consumers, as they are less sensitive to changes so demand will be less affected.
- Cut costs instead of raising prices. Reducing the costs of manufacturing the product will mean the business can make more profit without altering demand.
- Attempt to make the product more income inelastic. For example, moving the product from one which is perceived as a luxury or normal good to one perceived as a normal necessity good by changing its features.

Recession A fall in real GDP for two consecutive periods of 6 months. There is a large decline in economic activity across an economy (e.g. real income goes down as does retail sales and industrial output).

Income tax A percentage of their earnings a person pays to the government to fund public service such as education.

Exam tip

Make sure you discuss the disposable income of a consumer when answering an evaluative question.

Knowledge check 5

Give an example of when Aldi is most likely to see a fall in demand for goods based on consumers' income.

Summary

After studying this topic, you should be able to:
- analyse quantitative and qualitative research data in order to understand the position of the business in the market
- explain, calculate and interpret price elasticity of demand in a business context

- explain, calculate and interpret income elasticity of demand in a business context
- evaluate the impact of changes in price and income on business revenue

Sales forecasting

A **sales forecast** is a prediction of future sales. The process of **sales forecasting** is important for a business as it enables it to plan for the resources it needs to make and sell its products, for example how many staff or what production capacity is required.

A sales forecast can be used as the basis for a cash-flow forecast and a profit forecast, which the business can use to create a **budget**. It can also be used for market research, for example to estimate how much sales revenue will be generated at different prices for the product.

Factors affecting sales forecasts

Sales forecasts estimate how much money the business will make from future sales of its product. Such estimates can be affected by various factors:

- **Consumer trends.** Demand for the product can be affected by changing customer tastes and fashions. This may affect the market as a whole (market size) or a business's products specifically (market share).
- **Economic variables.** Demand for exports, for example, could be sensitive to changes in exchange rates, while sales at home will probably be affected if the economy slips into recession.
- **Actions of competitors.** For example, an improved product released by a competitor may reduce the sales of the business compared to the sales forecast. Such actions are hard to predict.

Difficulties in sales forecasting

- A new business will have no historical information about the sale of its product so will find it hard to predict the level of demand accurately.
- If the market is subject to significant technological change, today's rational prediction may look foolish in a year or two.
- As has been true of recent election opinion polls, market research may forecast success, but consumers may be too cautious to do what they said they would do.
- New competitors may enter the market after the forecast was made, overturning the underlying logic of the prediction.

Qualitative sales forecasting

A business can use **quantitative data** to create a sales forecast, for example using specific numerical information to estimate future sales. It can also use **qualitative data**, for example using the judgements and opinions of it managers. Qualitative sales forecasting techniques include:

- **Intuition**, where an experienced manager may have a 'hunch' or may make an educated guess that sales may rise even though the quantitative data show exactly the opposite.
- **Brainstorming**, where a group discussion takes place to produce ideas concluding in a sales forecast.

Sales forecast A prediction of sales revenue based on the historical number of sales made and current market research and trends.

Sales forecasting The process of predicting what a business's future sales will be.

Budget An estimate of income and expenditure for a business covering a set period of time.

Knowledge check 6

What should happen to a sales forecast for expensive handbags at the time of an economic recession?

Exam tip

Use any data given in an exam question to analyse and evaluate the ability of the business to make an accurate sales forecast. For example, who was responsible for the forecast and was there a risk of unconscious bias?

- The **Delphi method**, where a group of experts on the product provide their views on a range of issues, including market growth or sales growth. Their opinions are given in confidence with all parties being able to revise their forecast based on other views in the group. The group ultimately aims for a 'consensus forecast', one on which all experts can agree.

Advantages of qualitative forecasting
- It allows managers/experts to use their experience and expertise to make predictions that the historical data may not be able to take into account, such as knowledge of customer trends or the wider market environment.
- It can be used where there are few or no historical data available.
- It can be beneficial where the market is dynamic and changing all the time, for example in technology.

Disadvantages of qualitative forecasting
- It ignores a wealth of data that may act as an accurate template for future sales trends.
- Bias can exist in the personal opinions of those making the predictions, for example over-optimistic sales forecasts.
- The approach can be inaccurate and uncertain as there are no previous data on which to base it.

Calculating a three-point moving average

Moving averages can be used to calculate a trend, particularly where there are strong seasonal influences on sales or where there are random fluctuations of sales for no obvious reason.

Table 2 shows an example of a 3-month moving average with the sales for a shop as the raw data. The sales appear to be random as there is no obvious pattern so a moving average will help show a trend in sales.

Moving average One of a succession of averages of data, where each average is calculated by successively shifting the interval by the same period of time.

Table 2 Example of a 3-month moving average

	Raw data (monthly sales, £)	3-month moving total (£)	Centred 3-month moving average (£)
January	48,000		
February	57,000		52,000
March	51,000	156,000	49,000
April	39,000	147,000	47,700
May	53,000	143,000	46,300
June	47,000	139,000	45,300
July	36,000	136,000	44,700
August	51,000	134,000	

The moving average is calculated as follows:

- First, calculate the 3-month moving totals:

January to March = 48,000 + 57,000 + 51,000 = 156,000

February to April = 57,000 + 51,000 + 39, 000 = 147,000

And so on.

- Second, calculate the centred 3-month averages (centred means the mid-point of the 3 months' data):

February centred 3-month moving average $= \dfrac{156,000}{3} = 52,000$

March centred 3-month moving average $= \dfrac{147,000}{3} = 49,000$

And so on.

Scatter graphs, correlation and line of best fit

Correlation can help to explain data by finding a link between one set of data and another. The relationship between the two sets of data can be displayed on a **scatter graph**. For example, a business can use a scatter graph to compare its data on sales volume and advertising expenditure. If the scatter graph shows an increase in sales volume when advertising expenditure increases, this would indicate a positive correlation — if the business spends more on advertising, its sales volumes are likely to increase.

However, if the scatter graph shows only a loose or non-existent correlation between sales volume and advertising expenditure, expenditure on advertising should be halted as it is a waste of money at the moment. This situation can be seen in Figure 5.

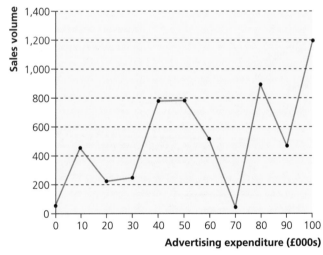

Figure 5 Loose correlation: are other variables important?

To make sense of the data in scatter graphs a trend **line of best fit** can be drawn, as in Figure 6. The graph shows that bonuses as a percentage of staff salary at John Lewis were at their best in 2008 with 215 shops, and that this percentage has reduced as more shops have opened — a negative correlation.

Line of best fit A line that goes roughly through the middle of all the scatter points on a scatter graph. The closer the points are to the line of best fit, the stronger the correlation.

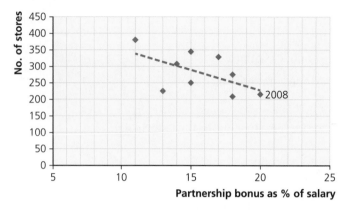

Figure 6 Correlation between number of John Lewis Partnership stores
and staff bonus payments, 2007–2015

Source: John Lewis annual accounts

When the data points on a scatter graph are all close to the line of best fit, as
can be seen in Figure 6, a strong correlation between the two sets of data is
indicated. This means the data are more reliable for the purposes of making
predictions. If the data points are spread far away from the line of best fit, only a
loose correlation can be shown and the data may not be reliable enough to make
any predictions.

The 3-month moving average in Table 2 shows the underlying trend for sales. Figure 7
plots the sales figures for each month (the 'raw data') and the centred 3-month average
sales, which clearly shows the trend for sales is downwards.

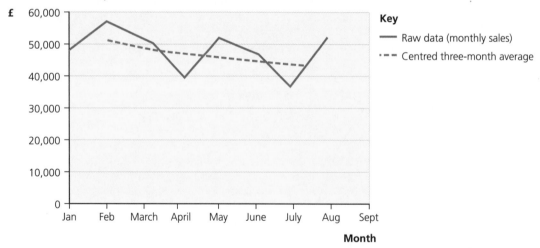

Figure 7 Underlying sales trends revealed by a 3-month moving average

Where **seasonal factors** are a key issue affecting sales, trends can only be identified
by looking at 12-month or four-quarterly averages, thus eliminating seasonal
variations. Figure 8 shows the four-quarterly moving average for the iPad with sales
peaking in 2013. After that the trend is downwards.

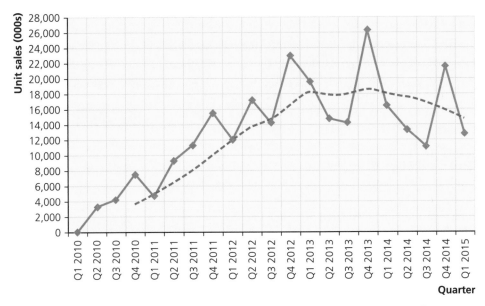

Figure 8 Global quarterly iPad sales since launch: raw data (solid line) and four-quarterly moving average (dashed line)

Source: Apple Inc. quarterly SEC filings

Forecasting by extrapolation means predicting the future from the trend line. This is based on the fact that the future is presumed to be similar to the past. The trend line can be extended to forecast future sales as shown in the example in Figure 9.

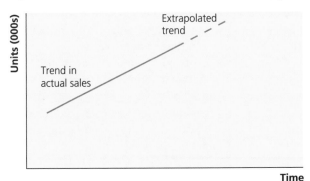

Figure 9 An extrapolated sales trend

This type of sales forecast can only be accurate if a business operates in a fairly stable environment. Managers should also look at potential future changes in the market to ensure such a forecast is realistic.

Knowledge check 7

Give an example of a situation when moving averages are a reliable way of forecasting future trends.

Time-series analysis

Time-series data consist of figures arranged in order, based on the time they occurred. The process of **time-series analysis** allows a business to identify the trend, which is the general direction sales are moving in, any seasonal fluctuations, which are the variations in sales that happen at regular times of the year, and any random fluctuations, where sales are unexpectedly very high or very low. Table 2 above is an example of data used in a time-series analysis.

Advantages of time series-analysis

- Historical data can be reliable in predicting future trends, particularly if collected over a long period of time.
- Seasonal fluctuations can be measured and compared over time to reveal patterns which act as a good basis for future predictions.

Disadvantages of time series-analysis

- Forecasting sales through quantitative techniques can be unreliable if there are significant fluctuations in the historical data.
- The process assumes that past trends will continue into the future, but this is unlikely in a competitive business environment.
- The process also ignores qualitative factors such as changes in tastes and fashions, or external shocks such as a recession.

Time-series analysis
A method that allows a business to predict future levels of sales from past figures.

Exam tip

Exam questions may ask you to calculate three- or four-point moving averages together with a line of best fit. It is always unwise, though, to simply extrapolate forward without reflecting on the risks involved.

Summary

After studying this topic, you should be able to:
- explain what is meant by sales forecasting and its usefulness, and the factors that can affect sales forecasting
- understand that sales forecasting includes quantitative and qualitative techniques
- calculate three-point moving averages
- create a scatter graph, line of best fit and extrapolate to predict future developments
- interpret information from time-series analysis
- understand that correlation can be positive, negative or non-existent
- explain qualitative forecasting techniques, including intuition, brainstorming and the Delphi method
- evaluate the usefulness of time-series analysis and the advantages and disadvantages of using qualitative forecasting

■ Analysing financial performance

Budgets

A **budget** is an estimate of income and expenditure for a business covering a set period of time. Individual managers may then be set budgets that represent their personal target or limit (e.g. 'my travel budget is £200 a month' means that is the maximum I can spend without having to ask permission from a superior).

A budget's main purpose is to help the business meet its financial objectives, but it can also be used to help establish priorities, allocate resources, motivate staff and monitor performance.

Analysing budgets and budget variances

Once a budget is set, the business then gathers information about its actual revenue and expenditure. It compares the forecast expenditure and revenue to the actual performance to establish any **variances**:

- **Favourable or positive variances** are where the actual results are better than budgeted. For example, revenues are higher, costs are lower, or profits are higher.
- **Unfavourable or adverse variances** are where the actual results are worse than budgeted. For example, revenues are lower, costs are higher, or profits are lower.

Variance analysis is the process of comparing the budget and the actual figures and investigating why there are differences. Whether the business needs to take action to address a variance depends on a number of issues. Was it a positive or adverse variance? Was it a foreseeable variance? How big was the variance? Are there any long-term trends?

For example, a positive variance such as higher revenues would not be seen as problematic in the way that lower revenues would be. With lower revenues, the business would want to look at the cause to see if there is a way to increase its revenues in the future.

Advantages of budgets and budget variance analysis

- Budgets allow a business to combine various sets of data and the expertise of its staff in order to predict the income and expenditure needed to meet the business's objectives, pre-empting any potential risks or challenges ahead, for example cash-flow problems which could be resolved by external funding planned well in advance.
- Budgets allow managers and stakeholders to monitor the business's performance against that predicted, making alterations before major financial problems occur.
- Budgets can act as a method of motivating staff through management by objectives with performance pay linked to achievements, for example reducing expenditure by 10% of the budget.

Budget An estimate of income and expenditure for a business covering a set period of time.

Variances The difference between the budgeted amount and actual amount for each item in a budget.

Knowledge check 8

Why might the *Independent* newspaper have had a positive budget variance when it switched from printing a daily paper to running an online website?

- Managers can choose to ignore areas of the budget with little or no variance from that planned, and focus their efforts on areas that require attention rather than on those that are running smoothly.
- Looking at areas of the budget with large variances means resources can be targeted on those areas that may give the greatest payback in terms of cost savings or revenue made.

Disadvantages of budgets and budget variance analysis

- Budgets are only as good as the data being used to create them. Inaccurate or unreasonable assumptions can quickly make a budget unrealistic.
- Budgets can lead to inflexibility in decision-making as they are seen as the ideal rather than just a plan.
- Budgets need to be changed as circumstances change, which can lead to more costs for the business.
- Budgeting is a time-consuming process and the larger the business, the more time-consuming it becomes. For example, finance departments can spend most of their time managing the budget.
- Budgeting can result in a business making short-term decisions to keep within the budget rather than making the right long-term decision which exceeds the budget.
- Employees may become demotivated if the business makes them accountable for variances in the budget that they are not able to control.
- If the budget is not set correctly in the first place, variance analysis may only show a small variance, masking potential cost-savings or gains in revenue.

The balance sheet

A **balance sheet** provides a summary of the assets and liabilities of a business at a particular moment in time. This means the business can see what it owns (its assets) and what it owes (its liabilities) at a particular time, usually at the end of every financial year.

Table 3 shows extracts from the balance sheet for the retailer Mulberry.

Table 3 Mulberry plc's balance sheet: current assets and liabilities, 2016/17

Current assets	£ millions
Inventories (stocks)	42.82
Trade and other receivables	14.66
Cash at bank	21.09
Total current assets	78.57
Current liabilities	£ millions
Trade and other payables	28.35
Current tax liabilities	1.25
Total current liabilities	29.6
Long-term liabilities	£ millions
Borrowings	0.0
Equity	£ millions
Share capital	3.0
Retained profits	69.96

Exam tip

Make sure you can analyse the variances between a given budget and actual figures. The examiner will give particular credit to extract-based examples of variances such as poor-quality production leading to materials wastage.

Exam tip

In the data-response questions particularly, you need to be able to evaluate the reasons for variances between a budget and the actual figures in an extract and suggest solutions.

Every financial transaction recorded on the balance sheet results in an equal and opposite change in the assets or liabilities, the so-called 'double entry' accounting system.

The components of a balance sheet include:

- **Current assets** — cash or other assets that can be converted into cash within 12 months of the balance sheet, for example stock, trade payables (amounts owed to the business) and cash in the bank.
- **Non-current assets** — assets that cannot be usually converted to cash within 12 months of the balance sheet, for example goodwill, property, plant, and equipment. An allocation, known as depreciation, is made on the balance sheet for property, plant, and equipment wearing out over time.
- **Current liabilities** — the amounts a business is due to pay out within 12 months of the balance sheet, for example trade payables (amounts owed to suppliers) and other payables, and current tax liabilities.
- **Non-current liabilities** — long-term financial obligations that are due in the longer term, usually more than 12 months after the balance sheet, for example any long-term borrowing such as a bank loan.
- **Equity** — any funds contributed by the owners or stockholders plus any retained earnings. Retained earnings are the net profits that have not been given to the shareholders, for example in 2016, Apple's retained earnings were $102.02 billion.

Current assets Cash or other assets that can be converted into cash within 12 months.

Current liabilities The amounts due to be paid out within 12 months.

Exam tip

Remember that both the current and acid test ratios are ways to measure the same thing – liquidity. If a company's liquidity is too weak, it may be unable to pay its bills, in which case the business may collapse.

Working capital

Cash, or **working capital**, is needed by a business to survive day to day and pay for such things as wages, supplies, taxes, long-term assets and other costs. Managing working capital effectively is important to the success of the business.

Working capital is calculated using the following formula:

working capital = current assets – current liabilities

Looking at the clothing retailer Mulberry plc's balance sheet in 2016/17 (Table 3), we can calculate Mulberry's working capital as follows:

working capital = £78.57 – £29.6 million

= £48.97 million

Mulberry plc therefore had £48.97 million available over and above paying off its short-term liabilities, so the company appears to have sufficient cash. However, the amount of working capital needed for a particular business depends on the nature of the products produced and the company's ambitions regarding future investment or product launches.

A business will also need to consider its **working capital cycle**, or the amount of time it will take for the business to convert its working capital into revenue.

An example of the working capital cycle is shown in Figure 10.

Working capital The cash needed to pay for the day-to-day operation of the business.

Working capital cycle The period of time between the point at which cash is first spent on production of a product and the collection of cash from the customer.

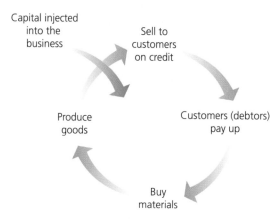

Figure 10 Example of the working capital cycle

Capital employed

Capital employed measures the total resources the business currently has available. It is calculated using figures on the balance sheet as follows:

capital employed = share capital + retained earnings + long-term borrowings

For example, looking at Mulberry plc's balance sheet in Table 3, it had no long-term borrowings but had share capital of £3 million and retained earnings of £69.96 million. Its capital employed for 2016/17 was:

capital employed = £3 million + £69.96 million + £0 million

= £72.96 million

Generally, the higher the figure, the healthier the situation of the business. In Mulberry's case, it had £72.96 million sitting on the balance sheet that could be invested in growth or used to pay off short-term borrowings.

Capital employed The share capital, retained earnings and long-term borrowings of a business.

Depreciation

On the balance sheet, the original cost of an asset is reduced by the amount of **depreciation** until the asset is regarded as no longer useful. Depreciation is calculated using the straight line method, where the same amount is deducted each year using the following formula:

$$\textbf{straight line depreciation} = \frac{\text{original cost of the fixed asset}}{\text{useful life of the asset}}$$

For example, if Mulberry plc purchased a packing machine for £10,000 with a useful life of 10 years the annual straight line depreciation would be:

$$\text{straight line depreciation} = \frac{£10,000}{10} = £1,000 \text{ per annum}$$

Depreciation appears in the profit and loss account as an expense and reduces the level of profit, which is useful when a business has to pay corporation tax. On the balance sheet, it allows for a fairer reflection of exactly what the assets are worth to a business, for example if it were to sell them.

Depreciation An amount deducted from the original cost of an asset to take into account the wear and tear in its use over time.

Analysing the balance sheet

The key to assessing the balance sheet is whether the business has sufficient current assets to cover its current liabilities, in other words enough cash to pay its bills. This means assessing whether the business's **liquidity** is satisfactory.

From the balance sheet, all stakeholders will be able to see the business's **current assets** — those easily converted to cash within 12 months, such as cash, stock and any money owed by customers for products (receivables) — and what long-term or **non-current assets** the business holds, such as property or machinery.

The balance sheet will also show any long-term **capital** the business has. This includes share capital and loan capital from bank and retained profits (also known as reserves). Share capital and reserves are owed to shareholders but do not require repayment so are treated separately. Added together they are called **total equity**.

Financial ratios

Return on capital employed

Return on capital employed (ROCE) is a financial ratio that tells us what returns (profits) the business has made on the resources available to it. ROCE is calculated by dividing a business's **operating profit** by its **capital employed**:

$$\text{ROCE} = \frac{\text{operating profit}}{\text{capital employed}} \times 100$$

ROCE is a good measure of the total resources that a business has available to it — the higher the percentage figure, the better the resources. To be of value, however, it needs to be compared with previous years to see if there is a rising or falling trend. ROCE can also be compared to the interest rates available for saving the money instead, to see if the risk is worth the return.

In 2016, Tesco's operating profit was £1,046 million and its capital employed was £18,034 million. Its ROCE was calculated as follows:

$$\begin{aligned} \text{ROCE} &= \frac{£1,046}{£18,034} \times 100 \\ &= 5.8\% \end{aligned}$$

This is a low percentage but the question is whether it is a poor return for investors, and comparing supermarkets may help. Looking at Table 4 we can see that Tesco's ROCE has suffered significantly over the last few years with the trend until 2015 being downward, in part due to the impact of discount supermarkets such as Aldi. However, 2016 has shown a slight recovery. But, if we compare Tesco's ROCE to Sainsbury's, we can see that Sainsbury's may be a better investment.

Table 4 ROCE: Tesco versus Sainsbury supermarkets

	2012	2013	2014	2015	2016
ROCE for Tesco	14.7%	14.5%	13.6%	4%	5.8%
ROCE for Sainsbury	11.1%	11.2%	10.4%	9.7%	8.8%

Sources: www.tescoplc.com and www.sainsburys.co.uk

Liquidity A measure of the extent to which a business has cash to meet its immediate and short-term obligations, or assets that can be quickly converted into cash to do this.

Exam tip

Extracts from a balance sheet could form the basis of an exam question, so it is important that you understand what the figures mean and who will be interested in them. When evaluating performance remember to discuss the limitations of the figures used.

Return on capital employed (ROCE) A financial ratio measuring what returns (profits) the business has made on the resources available to it.

Operating profit How much profit in total the business has made from its trading activities before any account is taken of how the business is financed.

Capital employed = shareholder funds + long-term liabilities. It is the amount of share capital and debt that a company has and uses. Shareholder funds = share capital + reserves.

To improve its ROCE, a business can increase its operating profit without increasing its capital, or maintain its operating profit and reduce the value of its capital employed.

Current ratio

The **current ratio** shows the business's ability to pay the bills due within the next 12 months. A ratio of between 1.5 and 2.0 is regarded as desirable. If the ratio is lower than 1.5, the business may struggle to meet its debts quickly.

$$\textbf{current ratio} = \frac{\text{current assets}}{\text{current liabilities}}$$

For example, where a business has current assets of £1,000 and current liabilities of £2,000 the current ratio will be:

$$\text{current ratio} = \frac{£1,000}{£2,000}$$

$$\text{current ratio} = 0.5$$

This figure means the business has £50 in short-term assets for every £100 of short-term debt. As the ratio is less than 1, this may indicate that the business will not be able to cover its short-term debts, particularly if this continues for any length of time.

Acid test ratio

The **acid test ratio** is a more severe test of a business's capabilities in meeting its debts. The formula is the same as for the current ratio but excludes the value of stock. This is because it assumes that stock may be perishable, may go out of date, or may go out of fashion or become obsolete. In other words, the firm may be left with stock it cannot sell.

$$\textbf{acid test ratio} = \frac{\text{current assets (excluding stock)}}{\text{current liabilities}}$$

A value of 1 is generally accepted as normal. Any figure less than 1 indicates there may be problems for the business as it may not be able to pay its debts. However, if the business trades in stock that has a very quick turnover, such as a supermarket, then the acid test ratio is of less value as a measurement of liquidity.

For example, a business may have current assets of £1,500, stock worth £500 and current liabilities of £500, so the acid test ratio would be calculated as follows:

$$\text{acid test ratio} = \frac{£1,500 - £500}{£500}$$

$$\text{acid test ratio} = 2$$

Gearing ratio

The **gearing ratio** measures the proportion of assets invested in a business that are financed by long-term borrowing. It is a way of measuring the long-term financial stability of the business.

$$\textbf{gearing ratio} = \frac{\text{non-current liabilities}}{\text{capital employed}} \times 100$$

The higher the level of borrowing the business has, the higher the risks it takes on. For example, interest rates on a loan could go up significantly and cause the business

Non-current liabilities
Debts payable by a business after 12 months, such as a mortgage or a bank loan.

to fail if its cash flow is too weak to pay those interest charges. However, if the business has good cash flow, **gearing** may not be such a large risk and may actually benefit the business in the short term. For example, getting a loan will reduce the amount of finance needed from shareholders and if interest rates are low and cash flow is good, the business could reduce its costs as the loan interest may be cheaper than paying dividends out to shareholders.

Gearing ratios can be interpreted as follows:
- A business with a gearing ratio of more than 50% is said to be 'highly geared'.
- A business with gearing of less than 25% is described as having 'low gearing'.
- Something between 25% and 50% would be considered normal for a well-established business which is happy to finance its activities using debt.

Gearing can be reduced by improving profits, repaying long-term loans, retaining profits rather than paying dividends, issuing more shares or converting loans to some form of share capital.

Gearing can be increased by focusing on growth, converting short-term debt to long-term loans, buying back ordinary shares or paying increased dividends out of retained earnings.

Interpreting ratios to make business decisions

Ratios help a business to decide whether it can afford to make various decisions, while investment appraisal or decision trees help it to decide whether the decision being looked at is worthwhile in the first place. A course of action can be financed in various ways, including using working capital such as cash, though this will worsen the liquidity of the business; borrowing from a bank or other source, though this increases the gearing ratio; or selling assets, which will be good for the liquidity and gearing ratios.

Analysing the trading, profit and loss account and the balance sheet to assess financial performance

The **trading, profit and loss account** can help assess the competitiveness of a business as it:
- Allows stakeholders/owners to see how the business has performed and whether it has made an acceptable profit (return).
- Helps to identify whether the profit earned by the business is sustainable ('profit quality').
- Enables comparisons to be made with other similar businesses (e.g. competitors) and the industry as a whole.
- Allows providers of finance to see whether the business is able to generate sufficient profits to remain viable.
- Allows the directors of a company to satisfy their legal requirements to report on the financial record of the business.
- Allows staff to gain an indication as to what any profit-related pay may be worth.

Gearing The proportion of finance that is provided by debt relative to all the long-term finance within the business (the capital employed).

Knowledge check 11

Will a reduction in interest rates be a benefit or a problem for a business with high gearing? Briefly explain your answer.

The **balance sheet** is important to:

■ **Bankers**, as they can look at the business's long-term borrowing when considering any further finance options.

■ **Suppliers**, as they can look at any outstanding money owed by the business and question why this might be if the business has plenty of cash and stock.

■ **Investors**, as they can look at whether the business has plenty of cash (a current asset), and particularly the trend for cash over time. This will help to insulate the business from tough times in the future and ensure its liabilities remain within reasonable boundaries.

■ **Staff**, as they may want to look at the accumulated profit of the business and how this has been distributed in terms of any profit-sharing scheme.

Considering business accounts in relation to previous years and other businesses

Business accounts, in isolation, provide information enabling a business to review and assess its current performance against its predictions and objectives. However, accounts can be much more useful to a business and its stakeholders when they track performance across a number of years. This can include:

■ Monitoring the balance sheet and the profit and loss account to ensure the business remains financially healthy and is capable of meeting its current and future objectives.

■ Looking for trends over time, such as the level of debt or the level of cash available to a business. For example, information from 3 or more years can give a good idea of particular trends, which managers can use to assess any action needed currently and in the future to improve business performance.

■ Looking at information from multiple years to identify problems with the accounts such as inconsistencies in ratios, allowing the business to find out what the specific problem is.

■ Tracking performance so that strategic decisions can be made, allowing a business to deal with future problems or to help grow the business.

Evaluating the financial position of a business

There are various problems in using accounts to measure the performance of a business:

■ Assets and liabilities can be valued and recorded in numerous ways on a balance sheet. This means that not only may one way give a more favourable outlook for a business than another ('window dressing'), but also that methods may change over time, both within the accounts of the business and with those who the business is competing against. This makes looking for trends and deciding whether a business is performing well much more difficult.

■ Accounts can only provide figures. They give no explanation as to why the figures are better or worse. They also only present a snapshot of the past, which gives no indication of how relevant the figures are for future business performance.

■ For new businesses or businesses which are expanding into new markets or products, previous accounts offer little help in predicting future performance.

Exam tip

To gain high marks when considering how a business is performing, remember to look at the financial, non-financial and other external factors. A business may look to be doing well, but when compared to the wider context this may not be the case.

Factors that can affect the accounts of a business

- **Window dressing**, which is presenting the accounts of a business in a way that enhances its financial position. This can be done in order to hide a liquidity problem from investors or to enhance profits so as to have a better chance of gaining finance.
- Changes in demand, which can have a positive or negative effect on the accounts. For example, if a product suddenly becomes successful, accounts may under-report the liabilities.
- **Inflation**, which is a sustained increase in the cost of living, and can significantly diminish the financial performance of the business. For example, retained profits may diminish its buying power due to sharp rises in inflation and/or the cost of raw materials.

> **Knowledge check 12**
>
> After production ceased recently of the Land Rover Defender, why might banks and other investors still be willing to invest money in a venture to build new, off-road vehicles, even though there are no business accounts? Briefly explain your answer.

Summary

After studying this topic, you should be able to:

- explain the meaning of budget variance, the main components of a balance sheet, working capital, capital employed and depreciation
- calculate budget variances, working capital, capital employed, depreciation, return on capital employed, current ratio, acid test ratio and gearing ratio
- interpret a balance sheet, return on capital employed, current ratio, acid test ratio and gearing ratio

- analyse budgets and budget variances, a balance sheet, trading and profit and loss accounts
- consider business accounts in relation to previous years and other businesses
- evaluate the financial position of a business
- understand that accounts can be affected by window dressing and other factors such as changes in demand and inflation

■ Analysing non-financial performance

Using financial measures alone will not accurately assess how a business is doing and whether it is doing well. Analysing the non-financial performance of a business allows for a much greater insight into the performance and trends likely to affect its success.

Non-financial measures

Customer attitude surveys

Customer attitude surveys can be undertaken either through quantitative or qualitative methods to assess the views of customers on a range of issues such as product quality or customer service:

■ Qualitative research, such as focus groups, aims to gain the opinions, beliefs and intentions of those surveyed, for example by asking why a particular customer decided to buy less or more of a product.

■ Quantitative research looks at larger groups of people and asks questions such as how often they purchased a product or how satisfied they were with the sales representative's approach in selling a product. This can done be through online or postal surveys.

The aim of customer attitude surveys is to allow the business to consider its strengths and weaknesses and to look at ways of better meeting its customer expectations.

Employee attitude surveys

Employee attitude surveys can be undertaken in the same ways as customer surveys, although the business may be looking to assess different issues. These surveys can look at staff satisfaction on a range of issues such as their role, their pay and their manager and senior managers. They can also be used to assess their training and development needs, the environment they work in, and their perceived career prospects.

Employee attitude surveys can help a business to:

■ assess the effectiveness of its policies and practice
■ identify low morale and how this might be addressed
■ facilitate change, for example lowering pay or raising targets

Market share

Market share is the proportion of the total market that is owned by a business or a product, for example Samsung had 34% of the smartphone market in the UK in 2017. A business can use a model based on market share, such as the Boston matrix, to assess what might be the best strategy for its product —such as investing in more marketing or creating an extension strategy. Market share can then be monitored to assess the success of the strategy.

Productivity

Labour productivity measures the output from each employee over a period of time. Productivity affects the costs of the business — if staff are more efficient, the unit costs are lower and the business is more likely to be profitable.

Comparing productivity levels can help a business to identify any problems and address them before they have a significant impact on costs. The business can look at whether updating equipment and machinery, improving production processes and raising staff skills and motivation levels have an effect on productivity. For example, it can check whether a new bonus scheme has improved productivity.

The business can also compare its productivity with its competitors in order to ensure it remains competitive. For example, in 2017, the Nissan car factory in Sunderland was recognised as the most productive car plant in Europe, creating 115 cars per hour.

Environmental record

A business's **environmental record** refers to the impact its operations and activities have on the wider world. Includes issues such as packaging, carbon emissions, waste disposal, a 'green' supply chain and sustainability. Sustainability is a business's ability to have little or no overall impact on the environment. For example, a business such as Amazon may use recycled packaging, energy-efficient equipment and obtain electricity only from renewable sources such as wind power.

There are many laws in place which businesses have to abide by when making and selling products. For example, under EU law, car manufacturers are responsible for recycling every old car they manufactured. A business will need to set targets for environmental issues that meet its legal and other stakeholder commitments. These targets can be measured and compared to previous years to determine how effective the business has been on its environmental record.

The importance of environmental issues to its customers means businesses often find innovative ways to reduce their costs. For example, the retailer Marks and Spencer has been operating its environmental strategy, called 'Plan A' for 10 years, and is now carbon neutral and sends no waste to landfill. However, some businesses like to advertise their 'green' credentials but actually practise little in terms of their impact on the environment. This is known as '**greenwashing**'.

> **Knowledge check 13**
>
> Give one example of a business that has made its environmental record a selling point for its products.

Summary

After studying this topic, you should be able to:
- explain how non-financial measures including customer attitude surveys, employee attitude surveys, market share, productivity and a business's environmental record can be used to evaluate performance

Aims and objectives

A **business objective** is a goal set by a business, usually in the medium to long term. It can cover the financial and non-financial issues important to the business's success.

Objectives set by the directors are referred to as corporate objectives. These are broken down into more detailed objectives for different functional areas of the business, such as production. The **functional objectives** are then broken down further into the different units or teams of the function. Ultimately these can then be translated into specific objectives for individual staff (Figure 11).

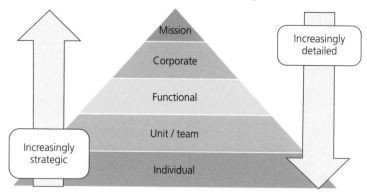

Figure 11 The hierarchy of objectives in a business

Corporate objectives

Corporate objectives are goals set by large businesses such as public limited companies. Large businesses often have many different stakeholders which means they need to set objectives which take into account their different needs and wants. For a public limited company, this includes shareholders, employees and customers.

A **vision statement** guides the business in its current and future actions. For example, Samsung's vision statement sets out a commitment to inspire its communities by taking advantage of its key strengths: creative solutions, innovative products and new technology. A **mission statement** is a short statement of a business's vision. So, for Samsung, its current mission statement is 'Inspire the world, create the future'. An **aim** is a generalised statement of what the business plans to achieve in the longer term. One of Samsung's aims is to become the largest mobile phone manufacturer in the world.

Corporate objectives set targets for the business as a whole. They are normally developed from the mission statement and are usually set by those at the top of the organisation such as the board of directors. Functional, team or individual objectives are set for different parts of the business, but all objectives must relate back to the corporate objectives so that each level of the business is contributing to these objectives.

Business objective A goal set by a business, usually in the medium to long term.

Functional objective A target for an individual department such as marketing, so that staff can ensure that the corporate objective is achieved.

Vision statement Sets out what the business desires in the long term and the key activities that will achieve this.

Mission statement A short statement of a business's vision and values which helps to set its aims and objectives.

Aim A generalised statement of what the business plans to achieve in the longer term.

■Strategy and implementation

Strategy, tactics and corporate plans

Strategy

Strategy is where the business is trying to get to in the long term, for example the markets it wishes to enter, the level of growth it wishes to achieve and the values and expectations it wishes to foster with stakeholders. Strategy is achieved using objectives. **Strategic direction** is the course taken by a business in order to achieve its goals.

Strategies can be put in place for different parts of the business:

- A **corporate strategy** is concerned with the overall purpose and scope of the business. It defines the markets the business chooses to operate in and where the business is trying to get to in the long term in order to meet the needs of its stakeholders. This can often be summed up in a mission statement.
- A **divisional strategy** is used by a part of the business to it help achieve the overall strategy. For example, Google has a division called Nest that builds smart thermostats and security cameras. Nest's divisional strategy will help Google achieve its corporate strategy of monetising products and opportunities.
- A **functional strategy** is used by a part of the business to help it achieve the corporate strategy. A function such as human resources develops its own strategy to ensure the overall strategy of the business is achieved, for example by ensuring there are sufficient staff with the right skills to make Apple's new headquarters function effectively.

Corporate strategy Defines the overall purpose and scope of the business to meet stakeholder expectations.

Tactics

Tactics are the smaller steps and shorter-term goals that help achieve the overall strategy of the business. Tactics involve plans and best practices, but need to be flexible enough to change depending on the success of business strategy. They often have specific start and end dates together with milestones that help decide how successful they have been.

Tactics The smaller steps and shorter-term goals that help achieve the strategy of the business.

Corporate plans

A **corporate plan** determines the goals the business wishes to achieve in the future and sets out how it intends to accomplish them. The corporate plan will:

- **Set out the business strategy,** including the mission and vision of the business. This will include looking at the opportunities and threats in the market the business wishes to operate in and setting realistic goals that reflect this situation.
- **Help plan and prepare the resources needed** to deliver the objectives, for example financial and staffing needs.
- **Set out clearly defined and measurable targets** for the business to monitor and control to ensure the objectives are met within the time limits stated. If the targets are not being met or are overachieved, the business will need to have in place a structure to resolve these issues.
- **Be reviewed each year** to evaluate performance and respond to any changes in the market and the economy to ensure the plan remains realistic and achievable.

SWOT analysis

The aim of **SWOT analysis** is to discover what the business does better than the competition, what its competitors do better than it, whether the business makes the most of the opportunities available and how the business should respond to changes in the external environment. The result of the analysis is a matrix of positive and negative factors to help the business plan a strategy. Table 6 shows an example matrix for the UK hotel industry.

Table 6 Strengths, weaknesses, opportunities and threats for the UK hotel industry

Strengths	Opportunities
■ Inward tourism has been rising steadily: a major strength in London and Edinburgh ■ The industry has a high, positive income elasticity, so as people get more affluent they use hotels more	■ British hotels such as the Ritz, the Savoy and Claridges are world-famous; this gives huge potential for growth overseas ■ After 5 years of prevarication, the British government committed itself in 2015 to cutting the high price of a visa for Chinese citizens; this should help boost tourist numbers
Weaknesses	**Threats**
■ Tourism is inherently a seasonal business, especially away from city centres such as London; this makes cash flow and capacity utilisation problematic ■ A lack of commitment by young English people means the industry is heavily reliant on immigrant – and therefore possibly transient – labour	■ Airbnb threatens to offer unmatchable price competition from individuals renting out their own rooms – an online threat to the hotel industry ■ Economic downturns hit the hotel industry hard; when the next economic recession begins, hotels will be among the hardest hit

In order to use SWOT analysis, a business needs to establish its current performance in the market compared to its competitors. For example:

■ **Internal strengths and weaknesses:** a business should prioritise factors that are important to its success over those that are less important. These include its brand image, sales and revenue figures, like-for-like sales, market shares and capacity utilisation. The key to prioritising the most important issues is to focus on the data that directly contribute to the business's corporate objectives. For example, in Table 6 for the UK hotel industry, a strength is more inward tourism in London. A weakness is the potentially problematic cash flow which could be clarified by looking at income and expenditure figures throughout the year together with hotel room occupancy rates.

■ **External opportunities and threats:** a business should focus on areas such as current and predicted population numbers for current and potential market segments, new legislation, technological changes, commodity prices and economic factors such as a rise in inflation or unemployment. In Table 6, opportunities can be seen for London's well-known hotels as a result of the government's loosening of visa restrictions on Chinese citizens. Threats include the rise of online companies such as Airbnb, whose technology allows individuals to rent rooms at comparatively low prices.

SWOT analysis A method for analysing a business, its resources and its environment. It is used to identify a business's internal strengths and weaknesses and its external opportunities and threats.

Knowledge check 16

Why might it be more effective to get someone who is not related to the business to perform a SWOT analysis?

Exam tip

When evaluating the strategy of a business remember that innovation and creativity can be just as important — many successful organisations are based on taking risks rather than spending too much time thinking about their strategies.

The key **strength** of a SWOT analysis is that it encourages a business to develop strategies to convert its weaknesses into strengths. For example, the hotel industry could create a technological response to Airbnb with rooms being offered at different rates on different platforms. This would provide a differentiated response to the identified weakness shown in Table 6.

However, a **drawback** of using SWOT analysis is that it may oversimplify the strengths, weaknesses, opportunities and threats facing the business. In addition, identifying the key issues can be time consuming and complicated.

Porter's five forces framework

Porter's five forces framework attempts to provide a simple way of looking at all the issues related to the changing competitive environment in which a business operates. The framework is summarised in Figure 13.

Figure 13 Porter's five forces framework

Source: Michael E. Porter, 'The Five Competitive Forces That Shape Strategy', *Harvard Business Review*, January 2008

Porter identified five factors that affect competition:

■ **Threat of new entrants** — the potential effect of a new business entering the market presuming it gains market share and rivalry increases. The position of a business is stronger the more **barriers to entry** there are in the market. Where barriers to entry are said to be high, it is harder for a new business to enter the market. Barriers to entry can include economies of scale, brand loyalty, up-to-date technologies and legal and pricing policies that a new business will need to develop before becoming competitive.

■ **Bargaining power of suppliers** — how much power a supplier has, presuming it sells its products at a higher price if possible. If the supplier is in a dominant position, then the price paid by the business for raw materials will be higher and so its profits will reduce. Factors that affect the bargaining power of suppliers include

Porter's five forces framework A model for analysing the nature of competition within an industry or market. It considers the threat of new entrants to a market, the bargaining power of suppliers and buyers, the threat of substitute products or services and the rivalry among existing competitors.

Barrier to entry A cost related to a business wanting to enter a market which is not incurred currently by those businesses already in the market.

the uniqueness of what they are supplying, the number and size of suppliers supplying the materials and the cost of switching to alternative sources of supply.

- **Bargaining power of buyers** — the extent to which customers are able to exert pressure and drive down prices. Factors that affect the bargaining power of customers include the volume of their orders, the number of rivals supplying the product and the cost of switching. Customers will have strong bargaining power if they are few in number, purchase a significant amount of the business's products, can choose from a wide range of suppliers or find it easy and inexpensive to switch to alternative suppliers of the product.

- **Threat of substitute products or services** — the effect of any product or service from a different industry that meets the same needs as the one provided by the business. For example, in the air transport business, substitutes might be cars, trains or buses. The level of the threat depends on issues such as the willingness of customers to switch, customer loyalty and the extent to which the alternative matches the business's product on price and performance.

- **Rivalry among existing competitors** — the intensity of competition in the market. This is the central factor in Porter's five forces framework (Figure 13) as it shapes the approach a business must adopt. If there is intense rivalry in the market, a business is more likely to adopt competitive pricing strategies, invest in innovation and new products, and increase its sales promotion and advertising. This all leads to higher costs and potentially lower profits. The intensity of rivalry is determined by the number of competitors in the market, the potential for market growth, product differentiation, brand loyalty, the availability of substitutes, capacity utilisation, the costs of entry and exit barriers. Table 7 shows the potential effects of differing levels of rivalry.

Table 7 The potential effects of differing levels of rivalry

Where the intensity of rivalry is low	Where the intensity of rivalry is high
A few businesses dominate the market	There are many competitors of roughly equal size
Branding is important to consumers	Products are relatively undifferentiated
Opportunities for market growth are available for all	Market growth is slow
There is little spare capacity	Capacity utilisation is low
Barriers to entry are high	Barriers to entry are low
There is no direct competition from abroad	Businesses face overseas competition directly

The five forces framework can be used by a business currently in a market to assess the security of its market position. Or it can be used by a business thinking of entering a market. Market research is needed to complete an analysis and market research companies such as Mintel regularly provide reports for this purpose.

The benefits of using Porter's five forces framework is that its acts as an excellent starting point for evaluating the current situation in a market and shows a business where it may be able to protect and grow its current product(s). However, the drawbacks are that it assumes market forces stay relatively static, which in many markets may not be the case. It also does not consider non-market forces, such as the impact of legislation, and can only provide a snapshot of the market or industry at a particular point in time.

Exam tip

When answering exam questions about Porter's five forces framework, recognise that it at best takes a snapshot of what is happening in a market or industry at a particular point in time. Therefore, it is quickly out of date, especially in fast-moving markets.

Knowledge check 17

For a business thinking about setting up in China why might it be more difficult to perform a reliable five forces analysis on the chosen market? Outline why non-market forces may be important in China.

Evaluating business strategy and corporate plans

The benefits

■ Business strategy enables a business to understand its customers better and attempt to anticipate their wants and needs.

■ It can help a business create a product that meets customer expectations but which can be differentiated from its competitors in terms of cost, innovation or quality.

■ Corporate plans give businesses certainty and confidence in their future approach to growth and success.

■ They can help businesses to look at various options and risks and create a structured method of ensuring the most positive impact on the business.

The drawbacks

■ Implementing business strategy requires collaboration between all parts of the business and even suppliers. Without this partnership, it will be difficult for the business to gain a competitive advantage.

■ A business will need to monitor its strategy carefully to avoid competitors gaining an advantage, and be able to change its strategy quickly or else risk losing any benefits gained.

■ Corporate plans are often little more than predictions of events and trends over which the business has little control. As a consequence, a lot of time and money can be invested into the plan with little reward.

■ For corporate plans to be effective, the forecasts they are based on need to be as accurate as possible.

Ansoff's matrix

Ansoff's matrix presents four alternative growth strategies in a matrix as shown in Figure 14.

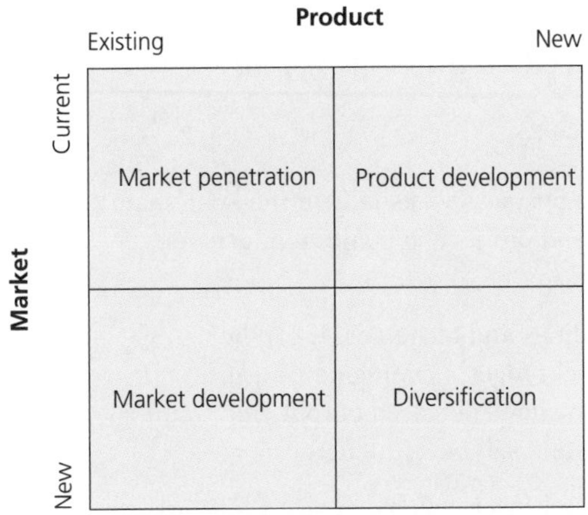

Ansoff's matrix A strategic marketing planning tool that links a business's marketing strategy to its general strategic direction.

Figure 14 Ansoff's matrix

The growth strategies suggested by the matrix are:

- **Market penetration**, where the business focuses on selling its existing products into existing markets. This could be done through maintaining or increasing market share, for example through competitive pricing, advertising or more personal selling. The aim might be to secure a dominant market position over competitors through aggressive promotion, penetration pricing and/or increasing the number of repeat customers through schemes such as loyalty cards. The benefits of this strategy are that the business already has a good understanding of the current market, its competitors and customer needs, so investment in new market research is limited. The risks involved in market penetration are low – but so too is the potential reward.
- **Market development**, where the business decides to sell its existing products into new markets. This can be done by entering new geographical markets, by using new distribution channels and using new pricing methods to attract different customers or create new market segments. If this works, it should bring in greater rewards than market penetration, but the risks involved are greater — think about opening the first Costa coffee shop in Mumbai, India, rather than opening it in Terminal 2 at Heathrow Airport.
- **Product development**, where a business aims to introduce new products into existing markets. The business may need to develop new skills to be able to create different products that can appeal to the existing market. This, again, is very risky: think about Walkers Crisps launching frozen roast potatoes.
- **Diversification**, where a business markets new products into new markets. This is a highly risky strategy as the business will have no experience in the market or the products. It must carefully consider the potential benefits against the risks before adopting this approach. If diversification is successful, however, the benefits to the business will be huge. And if one market is stagnant another may well be growing, insulating a business from an overall decline in performance.

The benefits of using Ansoff's matrix are that it gives an indication of the level of risk in pursuing the possible strategies for growth. It also shows the opportunity cost of each alternative and aims and objectives can be developed from each of the four approaches. However, the drawbacks of using Ansoff's matrix are that it is only a theoretical model and it does not take into account the activities of competitors.

Organic and external growth

Growth means expanding the sales revenue of a business — usually in the hope that profits will increase too. Greater sales revenues and profits can come from **organic growth** or **external growth**.

Organic growth builds on the business's own abilities and resources. It can be achieved by designing and developing new product ranges, opening new business locations, investing in new production capacity to allow increased output, and training employees for the new skills required to produce and sell new products.

External growth is achieved through a merger or takeover which can give a business fast access to new products or markets, an increased market share and help it to overcome barriers to entry in a target market. However, the costs of acquiring

> **Knowledge check 18**
>
> Thinking about the product life cycle, what element of Ansoff's matrix would be the best approach for a product extension strategy?

> **Organic growth** The growth in revenues and profits that arises when a business expands its existing operations rather than completing a merger or takeover.
>
> **External growth** Where the business attempts to grow by completing a merger or takeover.

or merging with another business are high and significant expertise is needed to combine the resources and visions of each business successfully.

The differences between organic and external growth are shown in Table 8.

Table 8 The differences between organic and external growth

Organic growth	External growth
Existing production capacity may be increased through investing in new technology	Production capacity may be increased through the merger or takeover of another business
New products may be developed and launched; new markets may be found	The product range may be expanded through a merger or takeover, and new product development may not be necessary
Growth can take longer to achieve as putting in place further employees, machinery and distribution resources takes time	Growth can be achieved relatively quickly as employees, machinery and distribution resources are already in place

An example of a business successfully using organic growth is Subway, the American sandwich franchise. In 2001, it announced plans to expand across the UK over 10 years. At the time Subway had only 52 franchised shops in the UK, however, by 2015, Subway had become the UK's largest franchised fast-food business with 2,000+ shops.

The advantages of organic growth are that it allows a business to **build on its strengths**, such as its brand and customer loyalty. It also allows the business to grow at a rate that is sustainable and manageable, perhaps financed by internal funds such as retained profits, making expansion less risky.

The disadvantages are that it may be **harder to build market share** if there is already a market leader, growth may be slow and economies of scale may not be gained as speedily as through external growth.

Mergers and takeovers

A **merger** is when two separate businesses of roughly equal size agree to combine into a new business. A **takeover** is where one business acquires a controlling interest in another business — effectively there is a change of ownership. The differences between mergers and takeovers are shown in Table 9.

Table 9 The differences between mergers and takeovers

Merger	Takeover
Usually occurs between two businesses of relatively equal size	Usually occurs when a larger business purchases a smaller business
Requires negotiation between the two sets of directors, and therefore a degree of agreement	Can be forced on a reluctant set of directors; a hostile takeover is where a larger business purchases a smaller business against the wishes of the smaller business's management team

Knowledge check 19

Why might external growth be a more appropriate approach for a business in a dynamic market?

Merger The combination of two separate businesses into a new business.

Takeover Where one business acquires a controlling interest in another business.

Mergers or takeovers are undertaken for various reasons, including to:

- acquire technological expertise
- reduce costs through economies of scale, in the hope of improving competitiveness
- move out of low or no growth mature economies such as the UK
- gain access to wider distribution networks
- diversify by investing in new products or new markets, such as India, to be less dependent on one product or market

A merger or takeover could be part of a business's growth strategy — part of its long-term business plan. To decide what its strategy should be, a business will use models such as Porter's five forces framework, portfolio analysis and Ansoff's matrix to see which option is the **best strategic fit**, i.e. which approach will fit most closely with the capabilities of the business and its corporate objectives.

Horizontal and vertical integration

Figure 15 summarises the different ways a business can complete a merger or takeover, by horizontal or vertical integration.

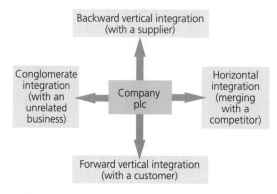

Figure 15 Horizontal and vertical integration

An example of horizontal integration would be Coca-Cola merging with Pepsi — both companies manufacture and distribute soft drinks for resale by retailers.

The advantages of horizontal integration include increased economies of scale, increased market share and market power, reduced production costs and reduced competition. The disadvantages include potential rises in unit costs due to diseconomies of sale, and the possibility of complacency among management and staff.

An example of vertical integration would be a film studio buying up a cinema chain to make sure its films are distributed widely.

The advantages of vertical integration include greater control over the supply chain, improved access to raw materials or manufacturing, and better control over retail distribution channels. The disadvantages include less scope for economies of scale as the business is operating at different levels of production. There is also the possibility of complacency if suppliers know you will always buy from them, or retail customers know you will always sell to them.

Knowledge check 20

Outline a potential problem for a larger business taking over a smaller business in the form of a hostile takeover.

Knowledge check 21

Why was Nokia, the mobile phone manufacturer, considered the best strategic fit for a takeover by Microsoft, a computer software producer?

Exam tip

Mergers and takeovers are a common exam topic so it is worth looking at some real life examples to see the approaches businesses such as Microsoft have taken — a takeover can simply be about getting rid of the competition rather than external growth.

Horizontal integration Where two businesses operating in the same industry and at the same stage in the supply chain become one business.

Vertical integration Where a business acquires another business in the same market but at a different stage in the supply chain.

A business may also undertake **forward integration,** which means a merger or takeover of a customer, or **backward integration,** which means a merger or takeover of a supplier.

Franchising and growth

Franchising is an agreement where a business (the **franchisor**) allows other businesses (**franchisees**) to sell its products or use its name for a percentage of the revenue generated. The business places the financial risks of setting-up on the franchisee and the franchisor can grow very quickly as a result. However, franchisees can find they are working very hard, while the franchisor is making most of the profit.

The benefits of using franchising as a method of growth is it provides easy access to expansion capital as it is the franchisee who will buy the outlet and provide most of the financing. The franchisor also gains access to motivated and talented people who will have a vested interest in making profits.

The drawbacks include the difficulties in finding the most appropriate franchisees to grow the business rather than expanding through the business's own employees, as there is a greater risk in the quality of the business being affected by poor franchisee management, which may negatively impact growth.

Rationalisation

Rationalisation can include selling or closing factories or different parts of a business, cutting costs, for example by moving to a cheaper location or by reducing staffing levels, or investing in machinery to reduce unit costs and increase production and productivity.

Location/relocation

Wages are one of the highest costs most businesses have, so relocating could potentially lower costs while still maintaining staffing levels. For example, staff are generally paid more in inner London so relocating to Birmingham may bring immediate savings. However, moving staff can be difficult and expensive due to redundancies and the hiring of new staff. It may also result in a loss of skills that may wipe out any potential savings from the relocation.

Transportation costs can be reduced by locating a business nearer to its supply of raw materials, particularly if the raw materials are heavy and used in large quantities. Alternatively, a business may benefit from being closer to its potential customers, for example, cinemas, banks or retail outlets.

Productivity

Increasing **productivity levels** benefits a business by reducing unit costs while maintaining quality, which can lead to a competitive advantage and ultimately greater profitability. For example, in 2017, the car manufacturer BMW announced that the new e-Mini will be built in the UK after the factory was judged to be more productive than those in Germany.

Knowledge check 22

Why might the US government stop a potential merger between Coca-Cola and PepsiCo? What might the two companies say is the benefit of such a merger to customers?

Rationalisation When a business reorganises its production in order to increase its productivity and efficiency.

However, the rush to achieve higher productivity can often result in staff being becoming demotivated due to unreasonable targets, leading to lower quality products and ultimately lost customers. Sometime a business may have to offer large financial incentives to increase productivity levels, which may reduce the positive impact of rationalisation.

Outsourcing

Outsourcing means getting a completely separate business to take on the work or part of the work of a business. Outsourcing is often done to take advantage of another business's specialised skills, cost effectiveness and worker flexibility. For example, Apple outsources the production of its iPhone to Foxconn in China.

The advantages of outsourcing include access to lower unit costs, specialised suppliers and services, and economies of scale. This allows the business to focus on its own core areas and to make savings by not spending on new production facilities.

The disadvantages include poor public and employee relations due to a loss of jobs, the higher costs associated with monitoring the quality of work, and a potential loss of customer service and brand recognition as outsourcing businesses may work for many other different customers.

Outsourcing A business gets another business to do its work for it, in the same or a different country.

Knowledge check 23

Why might a business such as Apple decide to spend $5 billion on creating its new 'spaceship' headquarters?

Exam tip

Try not to think of rationalisation and outsourcing as something a business only does once. Businesses often rationalise and outsource regularly as they grow.

Summary

After studying this topic, you should be able to:
- understand the relationship between objectives and strategy
- explain the meaning of strategy, the relationship between strategy and tactics, and the purpose of corporate plans
- apply SWOT analysis, Porter's five forces framework and Ansoff's matrix to a specific business
- evaluate business strategy, corporate plans and the usefulness of Ansoff's matrix to a business

- explain horizontal and vertical integration, organic and external growth, including franchising, mergers and takeovers, and their advantages and disadvantages
- evaluate the different methods that a business can use to achieve growth
- explain what rationalisation and outsourcing means and the factors that affect decisions about the location/relocation of a business
- evaluate the impact of location/relocation and rationalisation and the arguments for and against outsourcing production

■ Decision-making models

Types of decisions a business makes

Strategic decisions are part of a long-term plan of action to achieve business aims and objectives and are normally made by senior managers in a business. **Tactical decisions** are usually made by middle managers in response to opportunities or threats facing the business in the medium term. Tactical decisions are normally easier to change than strategic ones as they are less permanent.

Operational decisions are short-term decisions made by junior managers that are simple and routine. This could involve the regular ordering of supplies or the creation of a staff rota.

Figure 16 gives an example of how different parts of a business hierarchy may be responsible for strategic, tactical and operational decisions.

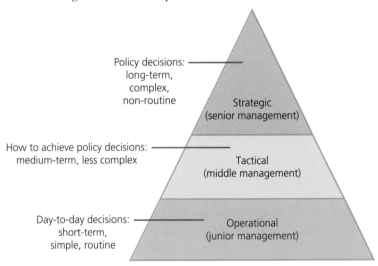

Figure 16 Examples of strategic, tactical and operational types of decisions made in an organisation

Making the right decisions is important to a business because:
- Once a decision is made, it is difficult to stop any processes that have been instigated, for example hiring new employees or purchasing new equipment.
- Decisions can have far-reaching implications, for example the success of a new product launch or the success of a venture into a new market.
- Wrong decisions can cause financial loss and ultimately result in business failure.

To reduce the risks when taking decisions, a number of tools and techniques have been developed to help businesses analyse different types of data. They can be split into two approaches:
- **Scientific-based (or evidence-based) decision making.** This is where a business makes strategic decisions after analysing and evaluating relevant evidence. Businesses will make full use of quantitative sales forecasting, decision trees and other methods that help quantify any decision being made. With the growth of the internet and computer analysis of large amounts of data, businesses can now automate certain decisions and react to change more quickly than their competitors.

■ **Intuitive (or subjective) decision making.** This type of decision making relies more on the experience and judgement of the owners and managers of a business. It often requires a more entrepreneurial, risk-taking approach. For example, Steve Jobs and Jonathan Ive were famous for their intuitive decision making at Apple.

Decision trees

Using a **decision tree** is a quantitative approach to decision making. Each decision is expressed as a number and any chance of something happening is expressed as a probability of it occurring. Decision trees are useful for analysing situations where a sequence of events needs to be followed to achieve an outcome, but the outcome is uncertain.

Constructing a decision tree diagram

A decision tree diagram looks a bit like a tree on its side with branches reflecting each decision and the different possible outcomes. Remember that for every decision proposed there is always the possibility of doing nothing instead.

Decision trees always start on the left and work across to the right. A decision is represented by a square, and a circle represents the probability or chance of something happening. Figure 17 shows an example of a simple decision tree.

Decision tree A mathematical model that uses estimates and probabilities to calculate likely outcomes in order to help a business decide whether a net gain from a decision is worthwhile.

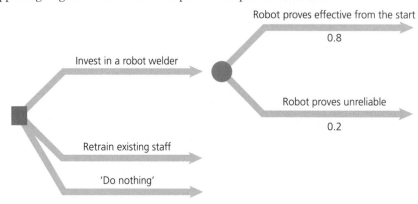

Figure 17 A simple decision tree

To create a decision tree:
■ A square is drawn on the left to represent a decision to be made.
■ From this square, lines are drawn out towards the right for each possible decision choice, and that decision is written along the line. For example, in Figure 17, the possible decisions are 'Invest in a robot welder', 'Retrain existing staff' or 'Do nothing'.
■ For each decision there will be outcomes that are uncertain and these are represented by a circle. In Figure 17, the circle gives two possible outcomes for the decision 'Invest in a robot welder', one of which is that the robot proves unreliable.
■ A probability is attached to each of the possible outcomes, the total of which must add up to 1. A probability of 1 means the outcome is certain to happen. In Figure 17, the probability of the robot proving to be effective from the start is 0.8 or 80%, which is much higher than the probability of the robot proving to be unreliable which is 0.2 or 20%.

- For each outcome, there is another decision to be made. Following the example in Figure 17, a business may have to decide whether to buy or hire a robot welder. Another square is drawn with lines representing each decision.
- If buying the robot has a net cash-flow cost of £1,000 per year while hiring costs are £800 per year, it may be better to hire. Figure 18 shows that the business has decided to hire the robot rather than purchase it, so the branch that is not taken is crossed out.

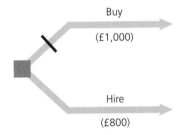

Figure 18 Example decision tree

Interpreting and evaluating a decision tree

In Figure 19, a business, Slade Farm, has to decide whether or not to launch a new product. Its research states that the probability of success as an outcome is 0.7 or 70%. As the probabilities must always add up to 1, the chances of the new product failing therefore are 0.3 or 30%.

Financial estimates for the cost of launch are £10 million. If the product is successful, it will create a positive net cash flow of £15 million. If it fails, the net cash flow will only be £3 million. If there is no launch, there will be no net cash flow.

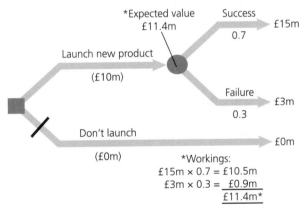

Figure 19 Slade Farm decision tree for a new product launch

At each circle a calculation needs to be completed — the probability multiplied by the estimated financial cost or income. In Figure 19, for example, we can calculate the cost for each outcome of success or failure as follows:

£15 million × 0.7 = £10.5 million

£3 million × 0.3 = £0.9 million

Total = £11.4 million

So the expected value for the circle in Figure 19 is £11.4 million, which is called a weighted average. This means that, on average, Slade Farm will turn the cost of £10 million for the new product launch into £11.4 million, a net gain of £1.4 million. This is better than the 'Don't launch' decision, so that option is crossed out.

Critical path analysis

Critical path analysis (CPA) is a technique that is used to find the cheapest or fastest way to complete a task. A **critical path** is a sequence of activities which if delayed will delay the whole operation.

Critical path analysis allows a business to:
- estimate the minimum time that should be taken to complete a task
- see how much time the complete project should take
- identify the earliest date at which later stages of the task can start
- anticipate any tasks that may cause delays to the project's completion

> **Critical path analysis (CPA)** A technique that is used to find the cheapest or fastest way to complete a task.

Constructing and interpreting a CPA diagram

There are two parts to a CPA diagram:
- An **activity**, which is part of a project that requires time and/or resources. For example, waiting for parts would be an activity. Activities are shown as arrows running from left to right (the length of the arrow is not important).
- **Nodes**, which are circles representing the start or finish of task. They are divided into three sections, each containing numbers. In the left-hand semi-circle, the node number is written, with 1 being the start of the process. The number in the top right quadrant is the **earliest starting time** (EST), the earliest time the task can begin. The number in the bottom right quadrant is the **latest finishing time** (LFT), the latest time that the previous task can finish without delaying the next task.

To create a CPA diagram:
- Always start on the left-hand side of the page and work across to the right. The diagram must start and end on a single node.
- Make sure you draw your nodes (circles) big enough to enter the three sets of numbers
- Draw arrows out from your first node to represent the first sequence of activities required to complete that task. All arrows must be activities, and the arrow lines should not cross each other.
- Draw another node to represent the end of that task, and then add more arrows to represent later activities for the next task, and so on until the project is completed.
- When you have drawn an activity do not add an end node straight away until you have checked which task is next.

Example

A crisp manufacturer decides to run a '3p off' price promotion next January. There are numerous tasks that need to be completed to ensure the promotion runs smoothly and these have been placed in the correct time sequence as shown in Figure 20. The diagram (or network) also includes how long each task is predicted to take. The longest path takes 70 days (14 + 28 + 21 + 7) so the work will need to begin 70 days before January.

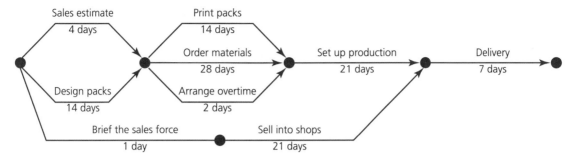

Figure 20 '3p off' network: activities

The next stage is to complete the nodes with the information on when activities can or must begin and end. The order of the activities helps with this. This is shown on Figure 21, the completed network.

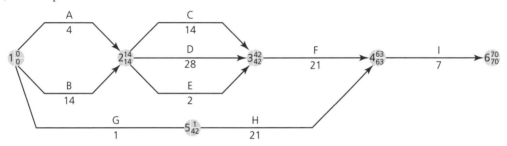

Figure 21 '3p off' completed network

- At the start of the project the first node always has 0 instead of 1 in the EST and LFT spaces.
- Activities C, D and E can only begin 14 days after the start of the project as that is when activities A and B will be complete. Therefore, C, D and E can start on day 0 + 14 = 14.
- Activity F can start on day 0 + 14 + 28 = 42.
- Therefore, the earliest the project can be completed is day 0 + 14 + 28 + 21 + 7 = 70.
- ESTs provide the earliest date certain resources will be available by and the earliest completion date for the whole project. Notice the 70 in the top right-hand quadrant of the last node, node 6, in Figure 21. This node also contains the LFT as 70 — the latest acceptable delivery time.
- The LFT in each node shows the latest finish time of the preceding activities. For example, node 5 shows that activity G must be finished by day 42 in order to have enough time to complete H and I by day 70.
- The LFTs for the activities are calculated from right to left. For example, Node 4 shows the LFT for activities F and H, task 6 minus task 4. This would be 70 − 7 = 63. The LFTs provide the deadlines that must be met in order to complete the project on time, the critical path and the **float time**.
- The critical path is the sequence of activities that take the longest time and determine the length of the project. In Figure 21 these are B, D, F and I. These activities cannot be delayed at all or else the whole project will suffer a delay.
- However, for activity C, a delay would not matter as this activity takes 14 days but there are 28 days available to complete it.

Float time The amount of time in a CPA network that a task can be delayed without causing a delay to the following tasks, i.e. it is spare time.

Identifying the critical path

By identifying the critical path, a business can focus on the really important tasks instead of focusing too many resources on those that are not as important. For the '3p off' price promotion, there are only four critical tasks that need careful management — designing the packs (activity B), ordering the materials (activity D), setting up production (activity F) and delivering the packs (activity I). Less resources and supervision are needed for the other activities.

The critical path can be found where the LFT and EST in a node show the same time and it is the longest path through those nodes. On a CPA diagram, the critical path is indicated by drawing two short lines across the critical activities as shown in Figure 22.

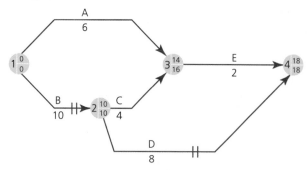

Figure 22 Indicating the critical path

Knowledge check 25

Critical path analysis looks particularly at the time taken to complete a project. Name two other important aspects of a project that a business should also take into account.

Float time can be used by the business to counter-balance the potential extra resources put into the critical path activities. The total float for an activity is calculated by subtracting the EST and the duration from the LFT:

total float = LFT (this activity) − duration − EST (this activity)

For example, the total float for activity A in Figure 22 would be calculated as:

total float (A) = 16 − 6 − 0

= 10

For critical path activities there will no float or spare time. For example, the total float for activity D would be calculated as:

total float (D) = 18 − 8 − 10

= 0

The business can then see which tasks need a lot of resources at particular times to complete and which tasks can either be delayed, take more time or need fewer resources to complete.

Exam tip

You may need to complete a CPA diagram provided in an exam question, or make changes to an existing diagram. You need to be able to identify the critical path and the total float, and be able to evaluate the usefulness of this approach to a business.

- **Perform complex calculations** on many different types of data and present the business with various forecasts for sales, revenue and costs to aid decision making.
- **Capture data on customer opinions** to provide a picture of how well the business is performing and what needs to improve to enhance customer satisfaction and ultimately sales.
- **Combine information in real time** across a number of locations and globally. This allows businesses such as the supermarket chain Tesco to be able to combine weather forecasting and customer spending data to instantly spot a trend for certain products, such as ice cream in hot weather, and order more stock to meet increasing demand.

However, the problem with IT is the sheer volume of data gathered and the risk that a business will lose some of its creativity by sticking too rigidly to computer predictions, their competitive edge.

Summary

After studying this topic, you should be able to:
- explain the types of decisions a business makes and the importance of decision making
- understand that decision-making tools can be scientific or intuitive
- explain the purpose of decision trees, critical path analysis and cost benefit analysis, and the benefits and limitations of each technique
- construct decision trees and complete critical path analysis diagrams, and interpret and evaluate the results
- carry out cost benefit analysis, and interpret and evaluate the results
- evaluate the advantages and disadvantages of using decision trees, critical path analysis and cost benefit analysis for business decision making
- explain the role played by information technology in business decision making

■Investment appraisal

Investment appraisal is a process used to determine whether funds given to a business for investment are likely to generate a profit. Various methods are used, all of which require a cash-flow forecast showing the investment over time and the predicted return on the investment.

The purpose of investment appraisal is to evaluate the attractiveness of a possible investment in quantifiable terms so as to lower the risks in taking an appropriate course of action. Understanding the risks depends on analysing the cash-flow forecasts, which helps to:

- assess the general feasibility of undertaking a project
- consider other approaches such as undertaking alternative projects or just leaving the money in a bank to gain interest
- reveal the level of investment required for the project to be successful, showing potential investors the probable rates of return and the risks

Payback

Payback refers to the amount of time it takes for a business to recover the initial amount invested. It is usually termed the 'payback period'.

Take the example of a business thinking of purchasing a machine to make widgets. It will need to invest £500,000 and it will want to know how quickly its investment will be repaid. According to the net cash-flow forecast in Table 11, the payback on the investment in the machine will be repaid by the end of year 4. The cumulative income at the end of year 4 shows a total positive cash flow of £500,000.

Table 11 Forecast net cash flows from a new widget-making machine

Year	Income generated (£)	Cumulative income generated (£)
1	100,000	100,000
2	125,000	225,00
3	125,000	350,000
4	150,000	500,000
5	180,000	680,000

If the annual net cash flows are constant over time, the following formula can be used to calculate the payback period for an investment:

$$\text{payback} = \frac{\text{sum invested}}{\text{net cash per time period}}$$

So if the new widget machine cost £500,000 and the net cash flow for the new machine was £100,000 per year, the payback would be:

$$\text{payback for widget machine} = \frac{£500,000}{£100,000} = 5 \text{ years}$$

Where net cash flows fluctuate over time, the following formula can be used to calculate how many months it will take to pay back the investment:

$$\text{payback} = \frac{\text{investment outstanding}}{\text{monthly cash in year of payback}}$$

For example, Table 12 shows a cash-flow forecast for a machine that is going to cost £40,000.

Table 12 Finding the payback period

	Cash in (£)	Cash out (£)	Net cash flow (£)	Cumulative cash flow (£)
Investment	—	40,000	(40,000)	(40,000)
Year 1	20,000	5,000	15,000	(25,000)
Year 2	30,000	10,000	20,000	(5,000)
Year 3	36,000	24,000	12,000	7,000

To work out exactly when payback is likely to occur in year 3, the calculation is:

$$\text{monthly net cash flow in year 3} = \frac{£12,000}{12 \text{ months}} = £1,000 \text{ per month}$$

$$\text{payback} = \frac{£5,000}{£1,000} = 5 \text{ months}$$

Payback The amount of time it takes for a business to recover the initial amount invested.

Knowledge check 26

What very simple question does payback answer for a business/investor?

The investment of £40,000 for the machine will therefore be paid back in 2 years and 5 months.

Payback predicts when an investment will be paid back and, more importantly, the point at which the business will start to make a profit on its investment. The best investments may be those with a short payback period, as this lowers the risk, and businesses can use payback to compare a number of potential options and then choose the investment with the fastest payback. Alternatively, some businesses may only invest if payback occurs within a maximum period of time, for example 24 months.

Average rate of return

The formula used to calculate **average rate of return (ARR)** is:

$$\text{average rate of return} = \frac{\text{average annual profit}}{\text{initial outlay}} \times 100$$

For example, if a construction business wants to consider its ARR on an investment of £2 million and its total net profit for the 5 years of the project is £1,350,000, the calculation would be as follows:

$$\text{average net profit per year} = \frac{£1,350,000}{5} = £270,000$$

$$\text{average rate of return} = \frac{£270,000}{£2,000,000} \times 100 = 13.5\%$$

Average rate of return is used to compare possible projects and interpreting ARR figures should take into account the level of risk and the period of time in which the return is forecast to take place. For example, the least risky investment for the construction business may be to place its money in a bank deposit account, but the ARR on such an investment might only be 2%. The ARR on the construction project, however, is 13.5%, so the opportunity cost of depositing the money instead of investing it in the construction project would be 11.5% per year.

Average rate of return (ARR) The average annual return on an investment for a project expressed as a percentage.

Discounted cash flow and net present value

Unlike ARR and payback, **discounted cash flow (DCF)** takes into account the profits from an investment and the time taken to achieve the return.

For example, £100 placed in a bank account for 12 months at an interest rate of 10% will give a return of £100 plus £10 at the end of the first year. Looking at this from another perspective, £100 will be worth 10% less in 12 months' time if it is not invested — the discounted value. Discounted cash flow helps to show the opportunity cost of money, sometimes called the 'time value of money'. This will show what the money is worth in today's terms, known as the **net present value**.

To calculate the DCF, you will need to know the time period for the entire project and the likely interest rate. The interest rate could be the current interest rate or it may be the minimum rate of return required by the investor.

Discounted cash flow (DCF) The process of calculating the present value of an investment's future cash flows in order to arrive at a current value of the investment, known as the net present value.

Net present value (NPV) The present value of all the money coming in from a project in the future set against the money invested today.

For example, if a business is considering whether to invest in either project A or project B, as shown in Table 13, the NPV can be established to decide which project is the better investment.

Table 13 Project A versus project B net present value

Year	Project A			Project B		
	Net cash flow (£)	Discount factor	Present value (£)	Net cash flow (£)	Discount factor	Present value (£)
0	(250,000)	1.00	(250,000)	(250,000)	1.00	(250,000)
1	+50,000	0.91	45,500	+200,000	0.91	+182,000
2	+100,000	0.83	83,000	+100,000	0.83	+83,000
3	+200,000	0.75	150,000	+50,000	0.75	+37,500
		NPV =	**+£28,500**		**NPV=**	**+52,500**

Both projects require a £250,000 investment and the rate of interest is predicted to be 10% over the life of each project. They also have the same costs and make the same money over the entire project. However, in Table 13, the NPV shows there is a large difference in investment returns with project B giving greater returns in the early years and a greater present value than project A.

Net present value gives a more realistic view of any investment, as it draws attention to the value of the return in today's terms. Different interest rates can be applied to reflect the expectations of different investors. After applying discount factors, the NPV could be positive, which may suggest it is a worthwhile investment, or negative, in which case the investment should be rejected.

The advantages and disadvantages of the investment appraisal methods

Table 14 shows the advantages and disadvantages of using payback, average rate of return and net present value.

Table 14 The advantages and disadvantages of different methods of investment appraisal

Investment appraisal method	Advantages	Disadvantages
Payback	■ It is simple to use and easy to interpret ■ It focuses on cash which is important to the everyday success of a business ■ It is straightforward to compare competing investments when resources are limited, and the opportunity cost of each	■ It may encourage short-term thinking about the investment ■ It ignores the qualitative aspects of a decision such as which option best meets the needs of customers ■ It ignores cash flow after payback has been completed and therefore cannot be used on its own to make a decision about the investment

Average rate of return	■ It uses all the cash flows over the life of the project ■ It focuses on profitability ■ It is easy to compare returns on a range of different investments, which aids decision making	■ The projected cash flows may prove to be inaccurate and that will affect the actual ARR ■ It ignores the timing of the cash flows which may only be positive towards the end of the investment ■ It ignores the opportunity cost aspect as it does not take into account the time needed to benefit from the investment
Net present value	■ It takes into account the opportunity cost of the money ■ It takes into account the timings and amounts of cash flow ■ It can be used to consider different investment scenarios in terms of interest rates	■ The calculation is complex so it is difficult to communicate to investors ■ The results can be misunderstood ■ Projects can only be compared if the initial investment is the same

Evaluating the viability of investment options

All three methods of investment appraisal are based on cash-flow forecasts, which may be inaccurate and affect the reliability of the appraisal process in assessing a potential investment. The more long-term the forecasts are, the greater the risk of inaccurate data, and therefore the more unreliable the appraisal process becomes.

Other factors also need to be considered such as corporate objectives, the business's financial position and whether the social and ethical responsibilities of the business are reflected in a potential project. The risks and uncertainty of each project also need to be considered.

Knowledge check 28

Why is investment appraisal of less value for a business whose corporate objectives focus heavily on being environmentally friendly?

Exam tip

Investment appraisal calculations come up regularly in the exams — practise them many times and make sure you can interpret your answers.

Summary

After studying this topic, you should be able to:
- explain what is meant by and the purpose of investment appraisal
- calculate and interpret investment appraisal, payback and average rate of return
- use discounted cash flow to calculate and interpet the net present value of an investment
- evaluate the advantages and disadvantages of the different investment appraisal methods to a business and its stakeholders
- evaluate the viability of investment options, taking into account quantitative and qualitative factors

■ Special orders

Special orders are where a business needs to decide if it should accept an order from a customer on special terms. Typically, this might be a large order placed by a retail business such as Next which is looking for a low price or a particular variant on a business's manufacturing process.

Accepting a special order depends on a range of factors, but a key issue is whether the costs of production will be covered by the amount to be paid. This will be decided by the cost per unit that the customer is willing to pay.

It is unlikely that the fixed costs of the business will be a factor as, for example, machinery will already have been purchased. Therefore, deciding to accept a special order comes down to whether:

■ the order increases the business's levels of variable costs
■ the company can resell the products
■ the order may lead to future sales

To assess whether the costs of production of the special order are worthwhile, a business will have to look at the product's contribution. Contribution refers to the surplus made on each product sold by the business, and it shows how many products need to be sold to cover the fixed operating costs.

Calculating contribution on a special order

Contribution can be calculated as follows:

> **contribution** = selling price – variable costs per unit

Taking a tool business as an example, a customer has asked if it can place a special order of 4,000 drills per year and is willing to pay £85 per drill. The tool business will need to spend an extra £10,000 on setting up the manufacturing process for this special order.

The fixed costs of manufacture are £420,000 and the unit costs per drill are:

■ Materials: £25 per unit
■ Direct labour: £28 per unit
■ Other variable costs: £12 per unit

The tool business normally sells its drills for £120 and at 80% capacity can manufacture 20,000 drills per year. The current contribution is:

> contribution = £120 − (£25 + £28 + £12) = £55 per unit

The breakeven point is:

> **breakeven** = $\dfrac{\text{fixed costs}}{\text{contribution per unit}}$

> breakeven = $\dfrac{£420,000}{£55}$ = 7,637 units (rounded up)

The amount of sales revenue currently needed to break even is therefore:

> 7,637 units × £120 = £916,440

Special order A one-off order requested specially by a customer.

Contribution The difference between the selling price and the variable costs of production.

Knowledge check 29

What would happen to contribution per unit if the selling price is raised?

As the tool business manufactures 20,000 units per year, the current sales revenue is:

20,000 units × £120 = £2,400,000

This means that, at 20,000 units, the tool business currently achieves a profit of:

profit = total revenue − total costs

profit = £2,400,000 − (£420,000 fixed costs + £1,300,000 (20,000 × £65 variable costs))

= £680,000

This now allows us to calculate the details of the special order and compare the figures as follows:

special order unit contribution = £85 price − £65 variable costs = £20 per unit

total contribution = 4,000 × £20 = £80,000

The total profit from the special order is therefore:

£80,000 − £10,000 extra set-up costs for the order = £70,000

Advising whether to accept a special order

In the tool business example, the special order created a total profit of £70,000. This was because the fixed costs were already covered by the normal level of production — the breakeven revenue required was £914,000 and the normal sales revenue was well above this at £2,400,000.

Clearly from a purely financial point of view, the lower special order price of £85 per drill generates a healthy profit for the business, so it would appear wise to accept the special order.

However, this may not be the case in other situations and there are a range of **non-financial factors** a business must consider before deciding to accept a special order, including:

- Will the special order lead to future sales that can make a positive contribution to the business's profits?
- Is the special order the best way to use any spare capacity? In the example of the tool business, the factory was said to have 20% of its possible capacity utilisation still available. Although a special order may make a loss, is it less of a loss than not utilising the spare capacity? Or does using the spare capacity interfere with the longer-term plans of the business?
- Will the lower selling price have a knock-on effect on other customers who now also want a lower unit price for their orders? The tool business appears to be making a reasonably healthy profit already, so this may be a key factor in whether to accept the special order.
- Are there any alternative contracts that are more profitable?

> **Exam tip**
>
> Try not to fall into the trap that special orders are all about whether there is a financial benefit to acceptance. A business may decide to suffer a short-term loss for longer-term profits or it may simply want to stop a competitor gaining the order.

Summary

After studying this topic, you should be able to:
- explain what is meant by a special order
- calculate contribution and advise on the appropriateness or otherwise of accepting a special order

Questions & Answers

The questions and answers in this section of the book follow a similar structure to your exams. There are extracts from business situations, data and a selection of all the different types of questions you will be asked to answer either in the WJEC or WJEC Eduqas A-level exams.

Immediately below each question there are some examiner tips on how best to approach it (indicated by the icon **e**).

For each question there is both a lower-grade answer (Student A) and an upper-grade answer (Student B). The commentary that follows each answer (indicated by the icon **e**) points out the answer's strengths and weaknesses, and how it could be improved.

Exam structure

The **WJEC A-level** qualification consists of four papers which are worth a total of 300 marks. This guide focuses on Unit 3 which lasts 2 hours 15 minutes and is worth 80 marks. The paper consists of compulsory data-response and structured questions. Questions can be worth 2, 3, 4, 5, 6, 7, 8, 9, 10 or 12 marks. You must answer all the questions.

The **WJEC Eduqas A-level** qualification has three papers which are worth a total of 240 marks. This guide focuses on Component 2 which lasts 2 hours 15 minutes and is worth 80 marks. The paper consists of compulsory data-response and structured questions. Questions can be worth 1, 2, 3, 4, 6, 8, 10, 12 or 14 marks. You must answer all the questions.

The subject content in Units 1 and 2 (WJEC) and Component 1 (WJEC Eduqas) underpin the context for Business Analysis and Strategy. For questions on Business Opportunities please refer to Guide 1 in this series, and for questions on Business Functions please refer to Guide 2.

Exam skills

Questions worth 1, 2 or 3 marks require knowledge of business terms. These questions may also ask you to calculate answers using formulae you have learned and data in the extract material.

Questions worth 4 or 6 marks require knowledge of business terms, specific application of the business term from the extract material and an advantage and/or disadvantage of the business term related to the extract material. These questions may also ask you to calculate answers using formulae you have learned and data in the extract material. The examiner will mark this type of question 'from the bottom up'. This means each mark is earned individually, so you get marks for an advantage, for example, even if you have not provided any context from the extract material. Context is anything unique you discuss from the extract in your answer. It must relate back to the question.

Questions worth 8, 9, 10, 12 or 14 marks require evaluation of the business term using specific evidence from the extract. The safest way to do this is to produce a strong, two-sided argument. You should also aim to make judgements about the business and the key terms discussed, as well as proposing solutions to business problems based on the stimulus material and your business knowledge. The examiner will mark these types of question from a 'best fit' point of view. This means that examiners will give you marks for the highest level of response you show in your answer.

For questions that ask you to analyse the advantages or disadvantages of a business concept, or ask you to assess how a business concept could be useful, the examiner requires you to focus on that side of the argument alone for the business being discussed, rather than giving an opposing view. You will also need to comment in detail about each of the specific factors in the context of the question stimulus material.

Technique when evaluating 12- or 14-mark questions

As these are the most challenging answers to write on the paper the examiner is looking for evaluation in detail. To help you gain the highest AO4 marks it may help to consider one of the following issues in your evaluation, known as MOPS, which stands for:

- **Market.** What are the characteristics of the market in which the business operates? How do these influence your conclusion? For example, Apple is in the smartphone market which is dynamic and fast-changing and therefore requires a lot of money to be spent on research and development to ensure the company keeps its competitive advantage.
- **Objectives.** What are the objectives of the business, and how do they align with the situation in which the business finds itself? How do these factors influence your conclusion? For example, Apple's objective might be market share, in which case making the most novel product, regardless of cost, may be of the greatest importance.
- **Product.** What products or services does the business sell? How might this influence your thinking? For example, Apple may bring out a cheaper iPhone in garish colours to capture more market share.
- **Situation.** What is the current situation the business finds itself in? Does this affect your conclusion? For example, with sales of smartphones peaking, Apple needs to find an extension strategy, such as selling to other global markets (e.g. India) to maintain/improve its market share, hence the need for a cheaper phone.

You need to read the extract and the question, and use the most appropriate element(s) of MOPS to help you consider the wider issues affecting the business that will influence the key issues in the question.

1 WJEC A-level

Extract 1

A new technology brand is attempting to convince London's super-rich to pay more than £10,000 for a smartphone with its first shop.

Sirin Labs, a start-up backed by $72 million (£50 million) of the chief executive Tal Cohen's own funding, investor loans and a large overdraft facility from Sirin's bank, is poised to launch the device into a crowded market in which Apple's iPhone dominates the high end.

Sirin will attempt to carve out a super-premium niche more than ten times more expensive than an iPhone by using military-grade security features and premium materials, such as precious metals and diamonds. Yet the smartphone at its heart will be based on Google's Android operating system, which is available to mobile phone manufacturers free of charge. Sirin has managed to source parts for its smartphones at a cost of £50 per phone.

The company hopes it can succeed in selling smartphones as status symbols in a specialised market where others have struggled, by making the phones to the customer's exact specifications. Cohen says the company is looking at a market size of 60 million, which includes 18 million millionaires. 'In every consumer market, about 2pc–10pc is high-end products. In mobiles, so far only 0.1pc–0.2pc of consumers have adopted high-end phones, so there should be at least another 1.8pc of this market attracted by a top-end product.'

Sirin Labs extract of assets for the month ending 30 June 2016

	£
Inventories (stocks)	50,000
Trade and other receivables	10,000
Cash at bank	500,000
Total current assets	560,000

Acid test ratio

Sirin Labs' total current liabilities for the month ending 30 June 2016 are £300,000.

Calculate the acid test ratio for the month ending 30 June 2016 to the two nearest decimal places. (3 marks)

The 'calculate' command word means you must complete a calculation in stages using data from the information provided.

AO2: for applying the acid test ratio formula using the correct figures from the information provided. An AO2 mark is available for stating the correct formula. This is worth up to 3 marks.

Giving the correct answer gains 3 marks.

Student A

$$\text{acid test ratio} = \frac{\text{current assets} - \text{stock} [a]}{\text{current liabilities}}$$

$$= \frac{560,000 - 50 [b]}{300,000 [c]}$$

$$= 1.867 [d]$$

ⓔ 2/3 marks awarded ⓐ The student states the correct formula for the acid test ratio for 1 knowledge mark. ⓑ The student misinterprets the figure for inventories (stocks) — it should be £50,000. This error means no mark is gained for this part of the calculation even though the other figures are correct. ⓒ The student places the current liabilities in the correct part of the formula to gain 1 AO2 mark. ⓓ The student incorrectly calculates the acid test ratio due to their previous error and gains no marks.

Student B

$$\text{acid test ratio} = \frac{\text{current assets} - \text{stock}\ \text{ⓐ}}{\text{current liabilities}}$$

$$= 1.7\ \text{ⓑ}$$

ⓔ 3/3 marks awarded ⓐ The student gives the correct formula and is awarded 1 knowledge mark. ⓑ The student gives the correct calculation of the acid test ratio to 2 decimal places for Sirin Labs which scores 2 marks in total.

Student A makes the type of mistake that can happen under the pressure of exams and misinterprets the figure from the information provided. If the figure is incorrect no credit can be given.

Student B has an excellent understanding of the formula. The calculation is correct for the acid test ratio. The correct answer alone is worth 3 marks. This is because the examiner presumes you could not have worked out the correct answer without knowing the correct formula and how to apply it, even though it may not be shown in a student's answer booklet. Showing your working out in the answer booklet is the best way to complete questions like this as even if you make a small error, you may still gain some marks.

Current ratio

Sirin Labs' current ratio at 30 July 2016 is 4.0.

Explain how using current ratio might help Sirin Labs manage risk.   (6 marks)

ⓔ The 'explain' command word means you must provide details and reasons for how and why the term 'current ratio' relates to Sirin Labs, giving a benefit or drawback as appropriate to the question, and justifying the point.

AO1: for giving a reason why current ratio might help a business manage risk. This is worth 2 marks.

AO2: for applying the current ratio to Sirin Labs using the information in the extract. This is worth up to 2 marks.

AO3: for explaining the benefit to Sirin Labs of using current ratio to help it manage risk. This is worth 2 marks.

Student A

$$\text{current ratio} = \frac{\text{current assets}}{\text{current liabilities}} \; \boxed{a}$$

Current ratio shows the business's ability to meet its short-term creditors. $\boxed{b}$

e **1/6 marks awarded** $\boxed{a}$ and $\boxed{b}$ The student gives the correct formula for current ratio and a brief definition but this only shows a limited understanding of the concept as it is not related to the question. One AO1 mark is gained for knowledge.

Student B

Current ratio shows the business's ability to meet its short-term creditors. $\boxed{a}$ An ideal ratio of between 1.0 and 3.0 is regarded as normal and this will help Sirin to easily assess whether it is able to pay its debts. $\boxed{b}$ In Sirin's case, the ratio is higher than 3.0 which could mean that the business has too much money tied up in stock. $\boxed{c}$ As a consequence, Sirin should try and reduce this risk, for example by spending more money on advertising its products in order to gain more customer purchases, thus reducing its stock levels. $\boxed{d}$ The current ratio helps Sirin to identify this risk and take action to reduce it. $\boxed{e}$

On the other hand, a ratio value of less than 1.0 would mean that it may not be able to meet its debts quickly. $\boxed{f}$

e **4/6 marks awarded** $\boxed{a}$ The student gives an accurate definition of current ratio gaining the first AO1 mark. $\boxed{b}$ They give a benefit for Sirin of using the current ratio gaining a further AO1 mark. $\boxed{c}$ The student correctly identifies the issue with Sirin's current ratio for 1 AO2 mark. $\boxed{d}$ and $\boxed{e}$ The student analyses a consequence of the current ratio and suggests a way of reducing the risk to the business for 1 AO3 mark. The point needs more detailed development for a further analysis mark. $\boxed{f}$ The student attempts to explain the risk of a lower current ratio value but as there are no further knowledge marks available and it does not relate specifically to Sirin Labs, no further marks are gained.

Student A scores only 1 mark (U grade), showing weak knowledge in answering the question.

Student B wastes time on giving a basic definition initially. However, a reason why the ratio would benefit Sirin is stated and developed, and the point is related to the context of the business. The point about advertising is not sufficiently unique to Sirin to gain further marks. Overall the answer would gain a C grade.

Sales forecasting

What is sales forecasting and how might it be useful to a business such as Sirin Labs? (9 marks)

e The 'what is' command phrase means you need to provide a knowledge-based definition of sales forecasting. For the 'how' command word, you need to supply an extract-based answer with advantages and disadvantages of the business concept in the question. The highest skill required is analysis.

AO1: for showing an understanding of sales forecasting by giving reasons why sales forecasting is useful or a definition of sales forecasting. This is worth a maximum of 3 marks.

AO2: for applying the usefulness of sales forecasting to Sirin Labs. You should use application from the context correctly. This is worth up to 3 marks.

AO3: for analysing the relative usefulness of sales forecasting in the context of Sirin Labs. This is worth up to 3 marks.

Student A

Sales forecasting is important to a business as it allows it to plan for the amount of products it will sell in a future period. a Sirin Labs will find this useful as it can forecast how many smartphones it will sell. b This will give the business a chance to look at consumer trends and the economy and base its sales on how many rich people will buy a mobile phone. c

Another reason is that by forecasting how many sales it will have for a future period, it can order enough stock to ensure it can meet the demands of its customers. d This means it will be able to ensure it makes a profit. e

---

e **4/9 marks awarded** a The student gives a definition which shows an understanding of sales forecasting and gains 1 AO1 mark. b They state how this might be useful in the context of the question using relevant application and gain a further AO1 mark and an AO2 mark. c The student gives further application of how sales forecasting will help the business so gains another AO2 mark. d The student attempts to give another benefit of sales forecasting but this is the same reason as in the previous paragraph so no further marks are gained. The student also attempts to show a consequence of being able to order enough stock, but again this is not sufficiently developed so gains no mark. e The student attempts to show a benefit of ordering sufficient stock, but this is not explained and is just an assumption so gains no further marks.

Student B

Sales forecasting is the process by which a company predicts what its future sales will be. a One reason this may be useful to Sirin Labs is that it can estimate how many £10,000 mobile phones it may sell. b According to the extract, Tal Cohen appears to have already looked at the market for such phones stating that there is a market of 18 million millionaires, and a sales forecast will try and estimate the number of those who will buy a phone from Sirin in London. c For example, as there are a lot of rich people visiting London in summer, the sales forecast will forecast greater sales and then order a sufficient stock of phones and premium materials to make sure Sirin is able to meet this possible demand. d As a consequence, Sirin will be able to supply its predicted customers with super-premium phones and make significant profits from each one sold, reducing the risk of missed sales and insufficient stock. e

Another reason why sales forecasting may be useful is to ensure that costly materials such as diamonds are only ordered and paid for when there is a potential sale. [i] As a consequence, there would be less money tied up in stock allowing for more working capital to be used for other purposes such as advertising to the millionaire customers. [g] However, as Sirin Labs is a new business which has just opened its first shop, it will find it difficult to predict potential sales as it has no past information on the demand for high-end mobile phones. [h] This means the business's sales forecast may not be that useful to start off with, which runs the risk of ordering a lot of expensive materials, such as diamonds, which may not be used as customers may not purchase the phone in the numbers predicted. [i] As a consequence, sales revenue may be lower than expected and there may not be enough cash to pay for bills. [j]

(e) **9/9 marks awarded** [a] The student gives an accurate definition of sales forecasting for 1 AO1 mark. [b] They give one use of sales forecasting using application for 1 AO2 mark. [c] The student develops the application in more detail to gain another AO2 mark. [d] The point is developed in the context of the extract to analyse another use of the sales forecast gaining another AO2 mark and 1 AO3 mark. [e] The consequence is developed with further context to show the benefit of sales forecasting to achieve another AO3 mark. [f] and [g] The student gives a further benefit in context gaining 1 AO1 mark, but there are no further marks available for application. [h] and [i] The student gives a well-developed analytical point about sales forecasting in the context of the new business gaining 1 AO1 mark. [g] The benefit is developed in the context of Sirin Labs gaining 1 AO3 mark. [i] and [j] The drawback is further developed but there are no further marks available for analysis.

Student A gives a good definition and develops this in context but the analysis for the two uses is theoretical. Broad assumptions are made for the benefits rather than being based on evidence from the extract, so only limited marks are gained. Overall, the answer would receive a C grade. Using the extract and understanding the requirements of the question are key to this student scoring well. Student B gives an excellent answer (A* grade) by applying the theory in detail to the business situation.

Extract 2

JD Wetherspoon started life in 1979 and became a plc in 1992. It now has 750 pubs which also serve food, and is the second largest pub chain in the UK. One of its reasons for success is that the pubs combine cheap food and drinks with opening hours that run from late breakfast to midnight. The largest shareholder is the founder and chairman Tim Martin, with 30% of the shares. Martin supported Brexit, which led to a tumble in the share price up to the referendum result but has now seen a significant increase from £6 to almost £9 per share in January 2017.

Profits reported to 24 January 2016 before tax were £36 million, down 3.8% compared to 12 months before. However, revenues for the same period increased to £790.3 million. Martin has suggested that this is because of higher staff costs such as rises in the minimum wage and also because pubs tend to pay more tax on alcohol than that bought from competitors such as supermarkets. Wetherspoon has started a programme of buying back its own shares, with the first purchase being for £39 million. Non-current liabilities for figures ending 2016 stand at £236.9 million and capital employed at £792.6 million.

Gearing

Using the data from the extract, calculate the gearing for JD Wetherspoon for the year ending 26 July 2015 to the two nearest decimal places. (4 marks)

(e) The 'calculate' command word means you must complete a calculation in stages using data from the extract.

AO2: for applying the gearing formula using the correct figures from the extract. An AO2 mark is available for stating the correct formula. This is worth up to 4 marks.

Student A

$$\text{gearing} = \frac{\text{capital employed}}{\text{non-current liabilities}} \times 100 \; [a]$$

$$= \frac{792.6}{236.9 \; [c]} \times 100 \; [b]$$

$$= 334.57\% \; [d]$$

(e) **0/4 marks awarded** [a] The student incorrectly states the formula for the gearing formula so gains no mark. [b] The student uses the correct figure from the extract for capital employed but places it in the incorrect part of the calculation so gains no marks. [c] The student uses the correct figure for non-current liabilities but places it in the incorrect part of the calculation so gains no marks. [d] The student incorrectly calculates gearing due to their previous errors and so gains no marks.

Student B

$$\text{gearing} = \frac{\text{non-current liabilities}}{\text{capital employed}} \times 100 \; [a]$$

$$= \frac{236.9}{792.6 \; [c]} \times 100 \; [b]$$

$$= 28.89 \; [d]$$

(e) **3/4 marks awarded** [a] The student correctly states the gearing formula for 1 knowledge mark. [b] The student uses the correct figure from the extract for non-current liabilities in the correct part of the calculation so gains 1 mark. [c] The student uses the correct figure for capital employed and places it in the correct part of the calculation so gains 1 mark. [d] The student correctly calculates the gearing to the second decimal place. However, as the percentage is missed off this gains no mark.

Student A makes the type of mistake that happens under the pressure of exams and misinterprets the gearing formula. If the figures are incorrectly placed in the formula no credit can be given. The student could have spotted this from the clearly incorrect percentage of gearing they calculated — it is not going to be a figure higher than 90%.

Student B gives the correct formula. The calculation is accurate and produces an answer that appears correct for gearing. However, the student has missed off the percentage sign so loses an easy mark. Showing your working out in the answer booklet is the best way to complete questions like this as even if you make a small error, you may still gain some marks. In this case, showing the working out has meant the student gains 3 marks rather than a D grade (B grade).

Extract 3

Research shows that the smaller the pub chain, the higher the growth, with some growing twice as fast as large chains such as Wetherspoon. The turnover of smaller chains has increased by almost one-third in the past 5 years. Growth has come from buying individual pubs and through unique selling points such as craft beers and restaurant standard 'gastro' food. For example, the chain Brunning and Price has grown to 54 pubs with pre-tax profits in 2015 up by 16% (£5.4 million) compared to the previous year.

Chief executive Richard Beenstock stated that 'we [Brunning and Price] have more freedom to experiment and respond to what the customer wants'. Beenstock believes this is the reason the company can transform establishments sold to it by large pub chains into profitable ventures. According to Beenstock, getting the pub offering right means it can increase turnover and profit. For example, instead of stocking national beer brands it supplies local brews.

Merger and takeover

Wetherspoon is considering inorganic expansion to meet its objective of becoming the market leader in pubs. It sees two options, a merger or a takeover of the chain Brunning and Price.

Analyse and evaluate which of these two options is the most suitable for Wetherspoon. (12 marks)

@ The 'analyse' and 'evaluate' command words mean you need to review the cause and effect of either a merger or takeover in detail, and the pros and cons of each using material from the extract. You will need to weigh up strengths and weaknesses to support a specific judgement forming a recommendation and conclusion. The extract should be used to provide application.

AO1: for giving a reason, a definition or some knowledge of a merger and a takeover, showing an understanding of each business term. This is worth up to 3 marks.

AO2: for good application of how a merger or a takeover would achieve growth in the context of Wetherspoon. You will need to clearly reference the extract to support your argument. This is worth up to 3 marks.

AO3: for giving good analysis of how the identified issues are important for the success of Wetherspoon. This is worth up to 3 marks.

AO4: for giving an excellent evaluation of the key factors affecting a merger or takeover assessed in the context of Wetherspoon. You will need to make a supported judgement about the business terms in the context of the question, and possibly provide a recommendation and conclusion about the best strategy for Wetherspoon. This is worth up to 3 marks.

Student A

A merger is where two separate business decide to become one single business, often to save costs and increase market competitiveness. a Brunning and Price is a small pub chain which specialises in unique beers and family dining. b If Wetherspoon merges with Brunning, the benefit would be in gaining Brunning's 54 pubs and customers straight away. c This means Wetherspoon would see an immediate increase in growth of its business. d Wetherspoon would also gain from the expertise Brunning has with its ability to experiment and respond quickly to customer wants. e

However, Wetherspoon may have to give the owners of Brunning a say in the way the new business is run and a share of the profits made. f As a consequence, there may be conflict between the senior managers of Wetherspoon and Brunning and Price that may reduce the overall strength of the brand image across the new business. g For example, Brunning may not wish to adopt the same discount approach that Wetherspoon is said to adopt and may want to keep each of its pubs unique. Wetherspoon may want to continue with its mass-market appeal of selling drinks and food at discounted prices. h

A takeover is where one business acquires a controlling interest in another business; effectively the takeover allows the business to be controlled by the new owner. i The benefit of a takeover to Wetherspoon is that it gets full control of any business decisions made about Brunning and Price's 54 pubs. j As a consequence, it could decide to develop the Brunning brand in a mass-market direction and still achieve very quick growth of its business. k In addition, gaining Brunning's loyal customers in the takeover may mean Wetherspoon is able to gain a more dominant position in the pub sector which may help it to reverse the 3.5% decline in profits it suffered in 2016. l This is the approach Wetherspoon should take in order to increase its market share quickly while enhancing the range of products it offers. m

e 9/12 marks awarded a The student gives an accurate definition of a merger for 1 AO1 mark. b, c and d The student relates the question to the context and develops a reason for and benefit of merging with Brunning which is one-sided but gains 2 AO2 marks and 1 AO3 mark. e The student develops the benefit to Wetherspoon with good use of context for another AO2 mark, but it is not effectively related to the growth objective so only gains 1 AO1 mark. f, g and h The student makes an evaluative point and develops this using evidence. However, the point is only weakly related back to the question and gains only 1 AO4 mark. i The student precisely defines a takeover for 1 AO1 mark. j, k and l A benefit of a takeover is developed with evidence, linking it to the objective of growth gaining 1 AO3 mark. m The student attempts to make a recommendation with evidence but has given no evaluation of takeover, and has not looked in detail at any of the MOPS elements, so gains no further marks.

Student B

A merger would mean that Wetherspoon and Brunning and Price would become one business. ⓐ As a consequence, Wetherspoon will immediately achieve its growth objective as it is gaining 54 new pubs and therefore a wider distribution channel as well. ⓑ As the owners of Brunning will be given a shareholding in the new business they are likely to play an active role in the development of the Wetherspoon brand, bringing their experience in developing pubs that respond quickly to customer wants, which may be a further benefit to the new business. ⓒ This would give Wetherspoon access to more niche market customers in the Brunning and Price chain that it currently does not gain sales from, and it could reflect this across the merged business giving Wetherspoon a further growth prospective. ⓓ As a result of this inorganic growth, there will be greater innovation through new skills and competences in the business at the same time as giving Wetherspoon more market power and the potential to increase its prices in the longer term, reversing the reduction of profits in 2016. ⓔ

However, a successful merger usually occurs between two relatively equal businesses and, looking at the extracts, Wetherspoon is significantly larger than Brunning with 750+ pubs compared to 54. ⓕ Also, Brunning does not seem to be the best strategic fit for Wetherspoon as it appears to be aimed more at a niche customers who enjoy experimenting with unique beers, whereas Wetherspoon is described as a discount chain. ⓖ As a consequence, there is likely to be significant opposition from Brunning to such a merger unless the business is able to retain a significant amount of its unique identity. ⓗ Wetherspoon appears to be dominated by its owner Martin, who holds 30% of the shares, so even if a merger took place, the short-term gains in growth may in the longer term be lost because of a reduced flexibility due to the new owners having different and conflicting corporate objectives. ⓘ

A takeover, however, would allow Wetherspoon to take full control of Brunning without a dilution of shares or a loss of control that normally occurs with a merger. ⓙ The key benefit of a takeover is the ability to make decisions independently of Brunning's owners, for example rebranding the pubs and benefiting from economies scale that the introduction of 54 new pubs would bring to Wetherspoon's buying power for beer. ⓚ However, whereas a merger may cost Wetherspoon very little in the short term, a takeover will mean it will have to pay for the controlling interest in Brunning, which may be expensive as the business seems to be steadily expanding and becoming more profitable. ⓛ Wetherspoon will also have to be careful that Brunning's customers are not driven away by, for example, losing the ability to experiment with unique beers. ⓝ

A merger or takeover will result in similar problems for Wetherspoon — too much interference with the Brunning brand will risk losing the benefits of growth. ⓜ The best possible approach may be to gain a controlling interest through a takeover, but to continue the Brunning brand in the short term as a separate business. Wetherspoon would be able to grow very quickly with the additional pubs, and could benefit from the knowledge and expertise Brunning's owners have acquired in a more niche market. ⓞ This would mean that Wetherspoon could start to develop more niche market features in its pubs, such as experimenting with unique beers and food, possibly attracting a new customer base and using premium pricing for such products to generate higher profits. p In the longer term, Wetherspoon may be able to rebrand the Brunning and Price pubs without losing its niche market customers, gaining a further competitive advantage that increases its market share to become the market leader. q

e 12/12 marks awarded a The student gives an accurate definition of merger in the context of the two businesses for 1 AO1 mark. b They then give a consequence of the merger for Wetherspoon, with evidence, gaining 1 AO2 mark and 1 AO3 mark. c, d and e The student develops the benefits of merging in detail, again with evidence, gaining 2 AO2 marks and 1 AO3 mark. f, g and h The student evaluates the effect of a merger by looking at Brunning's place in the pub market and making excellent use of relevant business terminology, gaining 1 AO1 mark and 1 AO4 mark. i The student develops the problems of a merger further making excellent use of the extracts to reach a conclusion and gains 1 AO4 mark. j The student now gives a benefit of a takeover, gaining 1 AO3 mark. k, l and m The student then compares a merger to a takeover, evaluating their relative merits for Wetherspoon with relevant evidence to gain 1 AO4 mark. n and o The comparison continues with the student giving a reasoned recommendation as to why Wetherspoon should choose a takeover but the maximum marks have already been reached. p and q The student goes on to look at the long-term strategy Wetherspoon could adopt for a successful takeover and the benefits of this recommendation in the context of the market but again the maximum marks have already been reached.

Student A gives a well-developed evaluation of a merger but only gives a one-sided argument for a takeover, and an attempt at a recommendation. Overall, a B grade answer.

Student B's A* answer makes excellent use of a wide range of business concepts and includes detailed knowledge of a merger and a takeover. It compares the strengths and weaknesses of both in the context of Wetherspoon's growth objective. A good tip for writing these longer answers is to compare and contrast both options together, which this student does well. The recommendation and conclusion looks at the different elements of MOPS in the short to long term as well as giving a strategy for implementing the approach. However, the student could have written a more concise answer and still gained full marks, giving them more time for other questions.

2 WJEC Eduqas A-level

Extract 1

The milk market is worth £2 billion per year in the UK (June 2011). Milk is sold in cheap clear plastic containers in litres at supermarkets, such as Tesco or Aldi. Typically little attention is paid to the packaging other than the name and type of milk. One litre of milk typically sells for £0.75 across most shops and has a shelf life of 2–3 days.

Cravendale is a successful brand of milk launched by UK company Arla in 2004. It uses a special type of filtering to remove more impurities from the milk than ordinary milk. Together with white plastic bottles and labels that stand out, the milk has a shelf life of up to 3 weeks. Cravendale has a sophisticated marketing campaign using television adverts and social media to raise awareness of its product, spending £5 million on advertising per year. Cravendale is sold in supermarkets at a premium price of £1.15 per litre. Arla posted profits of £8.3 million in 2012.

Tesco has now launched its own brand of filtered milk at the lower price of £0.95 per litre.

Income elasticity of demand

Evaluate the likely impact of an increase in consumer income on the demand for milk such as that made by Arla.
(12 marks)

(e) The 'evaluate' command word means you need to supply an extract-based answer discussing the advantages and disadvantages of the likely impact of an increase in consumer income on demand. You will also need to make a judgement on the likely impact on demand in the context of the question and include other relevant business theories. The extract can be used to provide application.

AO2: for good application giving the likely impact on demand in the context of Arla milk. This is worth up to 2 marks.

AO3: for giving good analysis of the likely impact on demand for Arla milk which should be balanced, detailed, well-reasoned and developed. This is worth up to 4 marks.

AO4: for giving excellent evaluation of the likely impact on demand for Arla milk. The advantages and disadvantages should be balanced and focused on a key issue. You will need to make a judgement with supporting comments and attach a weight to the value of each point made. This is worth up to 6 marks.

Student A

Demand is the amount of a good or service that a customer buys at a given price. (a) Demand for Arla's Cravendale milk has been high as it has made a profit of £8.3 million in 2012. (b) One advantage of an increase in consumer income is that consumers will buy more of the product. (c) The demand curve will shift to the right and demand will go up, resulting in consumers buying more of Arla's filtered milk. (d) If consumer income goes down then the demand curve will shift to the left and demand will go down (e). Cravendale milk will make more money if consumer income increases. (f)

e **3/12 marks awarded** **a** The student gives a definition of demand but in this style of question no marks are awarded for knowledge. **b** The student links the context of Arla's profit in 2012 to demand but this is a weak assumption and could be due to many other factors so gains no marks. **c** The advantage is correctly explained in the context of demand and the analysis gains 1 AO3 mark. **d** The student attempts to develop the advantage with some context and gains 1 AO3 mark and 1 AO2 mark. **e** The student is not directly answering the question here so gains no further mark. **f** This is simply an assumption with no development as to why Arla may make more profit and the use of 'Cravendale' is not sufficient to be classed as context as it is not used to answer the question so no marks are gained.

Student B

One advantage of an increase in consumer income is that, according to the theory of income elasticity of demand, consumers will buy more Cravendale milk. **a** This is because Arla's milk is likely to be regarded as a luxury rather than a necessity as it is more expensive to buy. **b** This means it is income elastic and therefore consumers who normally buy normal milk will switch to Cravendale when they have more disposable income. **c** A likely impact on Arla is that its profits will increase from its 2012 level of £8.3 million. **d**

However, the increase in Arla's sales will depend on the number of other competitors also operating in the niche market milk. **e** As the extract states, Tesco has also entered the filtered milk market with a similar product to Cravendale but at a lower price of £0.95 per litre. **f** This could be regarded as penetration pricing by Tesco which would have a negative impact on Arla of attracting customers away from Cravendale milk to Tesco's milk. **g** This would mean Arla's profits would not increase as significantly as if it was the only producer of filtered milk. **h** Arla should reduce its price so it can make more profit and gain market share from Tesco. **i**

e **9/12 marks awarded** **a** The student gives an advantage of income elasticity of demand and gains 1 AO3 mark. **b** The advantage is explained with the suggestion that as Cravendale milk is a luxury product, demand will increase as income increases. This suggestion includes sufficient context from the extract to gain 1 AO3 mark and 1 AO2 mark. **c** The student further develops the impact of rising incomes on Cravendale milk by linking it with income elasticity and gains 1 AO3 and 1 AO2 mark. **d** The student then links the point to a likely impact on Arla's profits using context for 1 AO4 mark. **e** The potential negative impact of other competitors in the market is introduced but this needs further development so gains no marks. **f** The student correctly links Tesco as a competitor using the extract but the actual effect is not yet mentioned so no marks yet. **g** and **h** The negative impact on Arla from Tesco is shown, with Tesco's potential pricing strategy identified, and the impact on both the market segment and Arla's profits evaluated, gaining 1 AO3 mark and 2 AO4 marks. **i** The student attempts to make a judgement as to what Arla might do to reduce the impact of Tesco on its milk sales but the point is not developed and shows little real link back to the question so gains no further marks.

Questions & Answers

Student A gives a very general advantage so fails to gain more than low marks for their analysis. The student's fundamental weakness is poor application to the context and poor evaluation of the key issues. This could have been a much better answer if the student had used the extract material better in their answer. It only gains a U grade.

Student B uses the extract well to give a benefit and a risk in context but drifts away from the question in the second part of the answer. The answer lacks a developed evaluation looking at a greater range of issues surrounding the question. The judgement and recommendation as to what Arla should do lacks any development so only gains low level evaluation marks. Overall, a B grade.

Extract 2

Pinewood Group is the number one film company in the UK. In 2015 it made record revenues of £75 million, £11 million more than 2014. Profits are also at a record high. The studio has decided to invest £200 million in doubling its size, due to high demand.

Ian Smith, producer of *Mad Max: Fury Road*, thinks Pinewood is successful because the government has offered companies tax incentives to use the UK studios instead of those abroad, together with its state-of-the-art skills in making films. In 2015 film and television production was worth £1.5 billion, with £1.2 billion of this coming from overseas countries such as the USA. The cost of making a film in the UK is high, as it requires highly skilled workers. However, producers are willing to pay these costs as Pinewood consistently shows a high level of reliability and quality in getting films made on time and within budget.

There are 36 sound stages at Pinewood along with 31 overseas sites that help the company maintain a competitive advantage in an increasingly globalised market. China is starting to become a serious competitor, with companies such as the Wanda group (the world's biggest cinema owner) looking to build 45 new stages that will compete directly with Pinewood. Wanda is a future threat, not a current one, as even though China has much lower staff costs, its skills are not yet sophisticated enough in film production. However, Pinewood will need to keep its standards up as within the next 10 years Wanda is likely to be a serious alternative in the film production world.

Extract 3

Pinewood has invested £200 million in a long-term expansion of its facilities so the studio can take advantage of increased international demand for film production in the UK. The money will be invested over the next 15 years, and Pinewood expects an average rate of return of 12% over the lifetime of the investment.

The money will see the studios adding 100,000 m^2 of new production areas, including 12 stages, several workshops and production offices. It is expected that the UK economy will benefit as £194 million of private investment will be made in the project, out of the £200 million in total. Forecast full-time jobs created will be 8,100, with a further 3,100 additional jobs in support services. The UK economy will benefit with an extra £36 million per year in taxes and £37 million per year in extra UK exports.

Extract 4

Pinewood's mission statement

- Continue to create the UK's leading film, television and media destination.
- Enhance our brand heritage.
- Exceed our customers' expectations through our commitment to professionalism, quality of service and offering sustainable advantage.
- Increase value for all our stakeholders.

From the Pinewood Group website, 9 August 2016

Extract 5

Profile of Ivan Dunleavy, Chief Executive of Pinewood Studios

Ivan Dunleavy is used to having to give up his offices for customers such as those making the next James Bond movie: 'we squeeze ourselves in'. Dunleavy states that making customers feel at home and giving them the right production facilities and staff is key to the success of Pinewood Studios.

He has been the chief executive of Pinewood Studios since 2000 and feels his modest and businesslike attitude to the Hollywood glamour allows him to stay focused on ensuring production crews get all the attention and expertise they need to produce the final glitzy experience of the cinema red carpet. Dunleavy says: 'we're there to provide services and a place to people who just want to get on with the job'.

Dunleavy believes that Pinewood's role is to empower film-makers to excel in creating outstanding films. It is in consistently reproducing this winning formula that has allowed the business to plan for the future and be successful. The chief executive aims to allow film producers (such as Ridley Scott on the set of *The Martian*) to harness the creativity and expertise of Pinewood, so that the film-makers and stars shine through, with Pinewood happy to stay hidden to the audience. Dunleavy admits he really enjoys the ever-changing nature of running a film studio, as do all his highly skilled staff. It is, he believes, a team effort at Pinewood and will continue to excel.

Decision trees

	Probability of success	Probability of failure	Estimated success in amount of profit/loss	Estimated failure in amount of profit/loss
Launch new campaign (B)	0.2	0.8	£15 million	−£2 million
Retain old campaign (C)	0.4	0.6	£7 million	−£1 million
Do nothing	0	0	£0 million	£0 million

Pinewood is looking at launching an advertising campaign for its new studio development and has partially constructed a decision tree to aid its decision making.

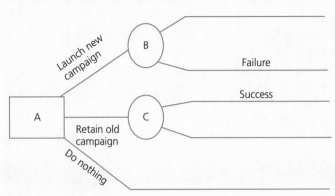

Decision tree for an advertising campaign for Pinewood's new studio development

Use the information in the table above to construct the remainder of the decision tree diagram and calculate the expected monetary rewards for options B, C and doing nothing.

(6 marks)

ⓔ The 'construct' command word means you must complete a diagram from the data and information provided. You should take into account any specific information provided in the extracts or context provided.

The 'calculate' command word means you must complete a calculation in stages using data from the information provided.

AO2: for constructing the remaining part of the decision tree diagram accurately (worth 2 marks), and for calculating and applying the probability formulae using the correct figures from the decision tree (worth up to 4 marks). An AO2 mark is available for stating the correct formula.

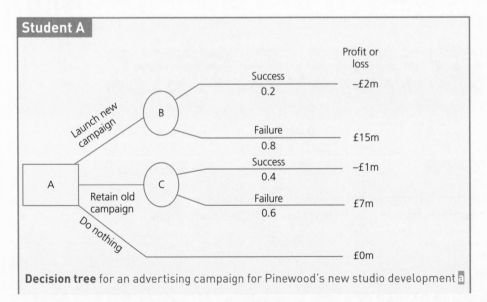

Decision tree for an advertising campaign for Pinewood's new studio development ⓐ

Option B:

Success	= £15 million × 0.2	=	£3 million	
Failure	= -£2 million × 0.8	=	-£1.6 million 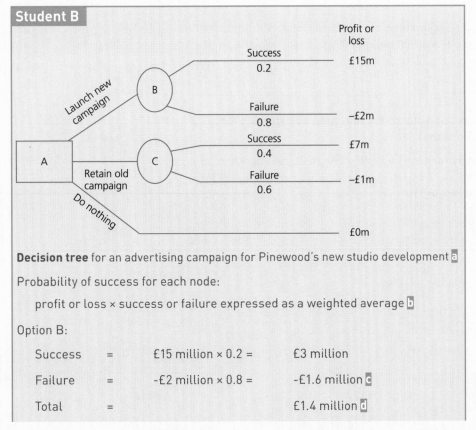 **b**	
Total	=		£1.4 million	

Option C:

Success	=	£7 million × 0.4 =	£2.8 million
Failure	=	-£1 million × 0.6 =	-£0.6 million
Total	=		£2.2 million **c**

e **3/6 marks awarded** **a** The student adds the probability of success or failure figures correctly to the decision tree for 1 AO2 mark, but confuses the profit or loss figures, assigning them to the wrong branches so gains no further mark. **b** The student uses the correct figures from the decision tree for success or failure to calculate option B and the weighted average, gaining 1 AO2 mark. **c** The student also uses the correct figures to calculate option C and the weighted average, gaining another 1 AO2 mark. However, no calculations are shown for the 'doing nothing' option, so marks are lost here.

Student B

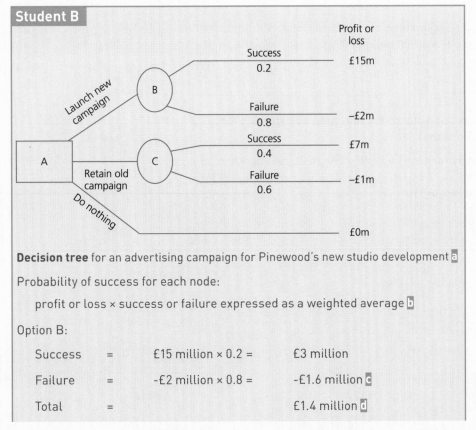

Decision tree for an advertising campaign for Pinewood's new studio development **a**

Probability of success for each node:

profit or loss × success or failure expressed as a weighted average **b**

Option B:

Success	=	£15 million × 0.2 =	£3 million
Failure	=	-£2 million × 0.8 =	-£1.6 million **c**
Total	=		£1.4 million **d**

Option C:

Success	=	£7 million × 0.4 =	£2.8 million
Failure	=	-£1 million × 0.6 =	-£0.6 million
Total	=		£2.2 million e

Do nothing:

Total	=	£0 million f

e **6/6 marks awarded** a The student annotates each branch of the decision tree accurately, inserting the correct figures for 2 AO2 marks. b The student states the formula for calculating the probability of success or failure for the different options as a weighted average and gains 1 mark. c The student uses the correct figures from the decision tree for success and failure to calculate option B and the weighted averages, gaining 1 AO2 mark. d The student correctly totals the figure for option A gaining 1 AO2 mark. e The student uses the correct figures to calculate option C and the weighted average gaining 1 mark. f The student correctly shows that the 'do nothing' option has zero value, but as the maximum number of marks has been reached can gain no further AO2 mark for this.

Student A does not follow the instructions in the question closely enough, missing out on 3 marks which they could have easily obtained (a D grade).

Student B has an excellent understanding of the calculations and produces the correct weighted averages. The student did everything that was asked in the question, including the doing nothing option to gain an easy 6 marks (A* grade).

Mission statement

Explain one reason why a mission statement may help a business such as Pinewood with its expansion plans. (4 marks)

e The 'explain' command word means your answer must include a detailed definition of the business phrase mission statement, relate this to the context and give a benefit or drawback appropriate to the question, justifying the point.

AO1: for giving a definition of a mission statement or a reason why mission statement might help with Pinewood's expansion plans. This is worth 1 mark.

AO2: for applying the use of a mission statement to Pinewood, using the material in the extracts. This is worth up to 2 marks.

AO3: for explaining the benefit of using a mission statement to help with Pinewood's expansion plans. This is worth 1 mark.

Student A

A mission statement is a short statement of a company's vision and values which helps to set aims and objectives. a A mission statement may help the business as it will allow it to look at the direction it wants to move in compared to the market and industry it operates in. b For Pinewood, the mission is to create the UK's leading film and media destination. c

e **2/4 marks awarded** a The student gives a definition of a mission statement for 1 AO1 mark. b The student gives a benefit of a mission statement which is sufficient for 1 AO3 mark. c The student quotes part of Pinewood's mission statement from the extract but as this is not related back to answering the question, it gains no marks.

Student B

A mission statement is a short statement of a company's vision and values which helps to set aims and objectives. a As Pinewood has just commenced a £200 million expansion of its business, b the mission statement may be used to communicate the purpose of this doubling in size to its stakeholders such as shareholders and staff. c For example, the mission statement says that Pinewood wants to increase value for all its stakeholders such as shareholders, d so this would communicate to its shareholders that the £200 million expansion plan was aimed at ultimately increasing the £75 million profits made. e

e **4/4 marks awarded** a The student gives a definition of a mission statement for 1 AO1 mark. b The student gives an application of the mission statement for the business, gaining 1 AO2 mark. c The student develops this application further and gains another AO2 mark. d and e The student correctly analyses a benefit in using the mission statement to help the business communicate positive messages to its shareholders for 1 AO3 mark. There are two further uses of evidence from the extract but as the maximum AO2 marks have been achieved, the student gains no further credit.

Student A scores 2 marks (D grade) but misses out on both application marks. Watch out for simply quoting from the extracts — marks for application are only awarded if you use the evidence to answer the question.

Student B's answer (A* grade) shows an excellent understanding of the use of a mission statement in relation to the business with particularly good use of evidence from the extracts to back up the points made.

Average rate of return

With reference to the data, evaluate the usefulness of using average rate of return for Pinewood Studios. (10 marks)

e The 'evaluate' command word means you need to supply an extract-based answer discussing the advantages and disadvantages of using average rate of return (ARR) for Pinewood Studios. You need to make a judgement about the usefulness of ARR in the context of the extract and include other relevant business theories. The extract can be used to provide the evidence for your answer and should be referred to. The highest skill required is evaluation.

AO2: for good application of the usefulness of ARR to Pinewood Studios. You should make clear reference to the extract to support your arguments. This is worth up to 2 marks.

AO3: for giving good analysis of the identified benefits or drawbacks of ARR for Pinewood Studios. This is worth up to 2 marks.

AO4: for giving excellent evaluation of the key factors affecting the usefulness of ARR, assessed in the context of Pinewood Studios. You should make a supported judgement about ARR in the context of the question, possibly with a recommendation about the best strategy. This is worth up to 6 marks.

Student A

The average rate of return (ARR) is a form of investment appraisal. **a**

$$ARR = \frac{\text{net return (profit) per year}}{\text{initial outlay.}} \times 100$$ **b**

The ARR for the proposed new studios at Pinewood is 12%, which is a good investment as this means investors providing funding for the development will get this money back for the 15 years that the project is expected to take. **c** However, this may not be as good as it seems, as an investor may be able to get a bigger rate of return from another project. **d** The ARR needs to be compared with other investments before anyone can decide whether or not it is a good project to put money into. **e** Therefore ARR can be useful for Pinewood Studios in showing potential investors how much they can gain from the project but there is an opportunity cost to this. **f**

e 4/10 marks awarded a The student gives some knowledge of what ARR is but not sufficient to gain a mark. **b** The student gives the formula for calculating ARR which is accurate and shows a theoretical response gaining 1 AO1 mark. **c** The student attempts to analyse the rate of ARR using relevant application but as the analysis is weak and based on assumptions this only gains 1 AO2 mark and 1 AO3 mark. **d** and **e** The student then attempts to evaluate the level of ARR but this has little development so gains only 1 AO4 mark. **f** The student attempts to draw a conclusion but it is undeveloped so gains no further marks.

Student B

Average rate of return (ARR) divides the average net profit from the investment by the initial investment cost to get the ratio or return that can be expected, expressed as a percentage. **a** One benefit of ARR for Pinewood Studios is that it provides a simple and readily recognised method to enable potential investors to see what return they could receive on the £200 million expansion. **b** For example, according to the extract, investors are forecasted an ARR of 12% so Pinewood can show that its expansion will give them better returns compared to other projects or current savings rates. **c** As a consequence, Pinewood will find it easier to raise finance for the expansion and possibly be able to secure a better rate of finance from investors than if it were to try and borrow the money from a bank. **d** Pinewood would also be able to look at the opportunity cost of any funds the business is looking to invest in the expansion, which could be the

£6 million over the £194 million coming from private investors, perhaps from retained profits 🅔 The ARR will help it decide if its money is better spent on the expansion or perhaps the relatively high costs of skilled workers and technicians. 🅕

However, ARR depends on how accurate the projected cash flows are. 🅖 As the £200 million expansion is expected to take 15 years, the risk is that predicted cash flows for so far into the future are going to be prone to inaccuracies. 🅗 For example, Chinese studios such those built by the Wanda Group, may take much more business away from Pinewood than the forecasts suggest, meaning the ARR may be significantly less than currently quoted. 🅘 The ARR may therefore not be useful to Pinewood in gaining investors for the project as those seeking to invest are going to wary of this problem and the heightened risks to their money. 🅙 Pinewood may find that it is unable to gain sufficient investors to fund the expansion which would ultimately impact on the business's ability to compete with global competitors. 🅚

Pinewood should use ARR but other measures of investment appraisal in addition to give investors as much information as possible to ensure funds are raised with as few risks to investors as possible. 🅛 For example, using discounted cash flow would be a more accurate measurement of the risk which investors would have greater confidence in when considering the project as it calculates the present value of an investment's future cash flows in order to arrive at a current value of the investment, known as the net present value. 🅜 With such a huge amount of investment required over 15 years, Pinewood will need to supply detailed investment appraisal information to ensure the project is successfully funded and its competitive edge is maintained so ARR will need to be one of a range of tools that are used to ensure the investment is successfully obtained. 🅝

🅔 10/10 marks awarded 🅐 The student gives a definition of ARR gaining 1 AO1 mark for a limited theoretical response. 🅑 and 🅒 The student uses the extracts to show a consequence of the benefit of ARR which is developed with a good example for 1 AO2 mark and 1 AO3 mark. 🅓 The student develops the consequence of ARR with relevance to Pinewood to gain 1 AO3 mark. 🅔 and 🅕 Another benefit of ARR is developed with good use of the evidence but it is one-sided so gains only 1 AO4 mark. 🅖, 🅗, 🅘, 🅙 and 🅚 The student evaluates ARR using excellent evidence from the extract gaining 2 AO4 marks. 🅛 and 🅜 The student gives a reasoned judgement on the usefulness of ARR and makes a clear suggestion as to a method of investment appraisal that may be more effective with reasons why supported with evidence, gaining 3 AO4 marks. 🅝 The student develops the judgement to form a reasoned conclusion that looks at the context of ARR and the MOPS elements, but the student has already scored maximum marks so cannot gain credit for this.

Student A gives a poorly developed answer (E grade). Higher-level skills such as using the extract to answer the question are evidenced but the answer needs to be expanded on to score more highly.

Student B makes excellent use of a wide range of business concepts and shows an excellent level of analysis of the extracts to give a wide-ranging evaluation in answer to the question (A* grade).

Corporate objectives

Discuss the importance of corporate objectives for a business such as Pinewood Studios.

(12 marks)

ⓔ The 'discuss' command word means you should examine the importance of corporate objectives in detail, addressing advantages and disadvantages with an extract-based answer. You will need to make a judgement and conclusion about the importance of corporate objectives in the context of the extract and include other relevant business theories.

AO1: for showing a good understanding of corporate objectives by for example, defining corporate objectives. This is worth up to 2 marks.

AO2: for good application of corporate objectives in the context of Pinewood Studios. This is worth up to 2 marks.

AO3: for excellent analysis of why corporate objectives are important to Pinewood Studios. You should discuss advantages and disadvantages and correctly apply them to the business context. This is worth up to 4 marks.

AO4: for giving an excellent evaluation of the importance of corporate objectives to Pinewood Studios. The advantages and disadvantages you identify should link together and your evaluation should be coherent and well developed. You should make a judgement about the importance of corporate objectives in the context of the question. This is worth up to 4 marks.

Student A

Corporate objectives are goals set by a large business such as a public limited company. ⓐ Corporate objectives are important because Extract 2 says that Pinewood's profits are up and the business is investing £200 million in an expansion project, indicating that it has a clear set of goals that its staff understand and are able to work towards. ⓑ Without corporate objectives, Pinewood would not be able have a clear plan to help it fight the current globalisation of film-making. ⓒ Corporate objectives encourage Pinewood to be constantly assessing the opportunities and threats within its chosen market, ensuring that lower-cost competitors such as Wanda find it difficult to gain market share. ⓓ

However, corporate objectives may not be so important to Pinewood as it is already extremely successful with 36 film stages in the UK and 31 overseas. ⓔ With films being made there such as the Star Wars movies, Pinewood can better use the money it might spend on creating corporate objectives to pay for more important projects such as hiring more staff. ⓕ This would be a better strategy than wasting time on corporate objectives and means Pinewood can 'exceed our customers' expectations'. ⓖ

In conclusion, while corporate objectives may be important to businesses that are new to a market, for a well-established film studio such as Pinewood, it is better off investing in projects to enhance its competitive advantage. ⓗ

ⓔ 9/12 marks awarded ⓐ The student gives a definition of corporate objectives for 1 AO1 mark. ⓑ The student gives a reason why corporate objectives are important in context for 1 AO2 mark and 1 AO3 mark. ⓒ The student develops the analytical point and gains 1 AO3 mark, however the context used is limited so gains no further mark. ⓓ The student gives a further benefit of corporate objectives with good use of the extract for 1 AO3 mark and 1 AO2 mark. ⓔ, ⓕ and ⓖ The student then attempts to evaluate why corporate objectives are not so important, showing understanding for 1 AO1 mark but limited evaluation so only gaining 1 AO4 mark. This is done using evidence from the extracts, so gains 1 AO2 mark. ⓗ The student attempts a conclusion which is weak and a repetition of earlier points, gaining no further credit.

Student B

Corporate objectives are goals set by a large business such as a public limited company. ⓐ Corporate objectives are important to Pinewood as they help it in the forward planning of the £200 million expansion project, indicating that it has a clear set of goals that stakeholders such as the 8,000 staff and investors can work towards. ⓑ For example, without clear goals and targets setting out the long-term scheme, Pinewood is unlikely to gain the private investment of £194 million required to make the project a success. ⓒ As a consequence, Pinewood would risk not being able expand its studios over the next 15 years, risking missing out on increasing revenues above the £75 million in 2015. And this could also diminish its competitive advantage compared to new competitors such as Wanda. ⓓ

However, corporate objectives can be unclear and may not be interpreted by managers within Pinewood in a way that guarantees the most efficient use of the £200 million. ⓔ Creative staff such as those that would be working on new film stages may interpret 'exceeding customer expectations' in a different way to what senior managers envisaged when creating the objectives. ⓕ This would produce a potential diseconomy of scale and risk the objectives becoming ineffective in achieving growth over the 15-year period of the expansion. ⓖ

However, the creation of corporate objectives does allow Pinewood managers at all levels, from Dunleavy downwards, to monitor the performance of the business against the targets and objectives set. ⓗ As a consequence, if there are any miscommunications with staff over how and what Pinewood wishes to achieve, this can be rectified. ⓘ For example, if the objectives were broken into more manageable targets such as building 12 stages each year, then if this was not achieved, Pinewood would be able to address the issues at an early stage, ensuring time and money is spent efficiently and lowering the risks of failure significantly. ⓙ

Corporate objectives may not be so important to Pinewood as it is a creative and fast-moving industry where staff are likely to work largely independently, meaning such objectives may actually risk stunting innovation and the skills that appear to be the draw for US film-makers. ⓚ If staff see that large stages are no longer the way forward, and spot a more lucrative innovation such as virtual reality, corporate objectives may actually reduce Pinewood's USP and in the longer term drive customers to other studios who have innovated such as Wanda, risking significant losses. ⓛ

> Without corporate objectives, a large organisation such as Pinewood, which is spread over 67 film stages worldwide, would be at great risk of long-term failure due to a lack of clear direction and targets. m Corporate objectives are therefore of critical importance to the success of the studio and Pinewood can reduce the risk associated with such targets by using techniques such as SMART, n for example, by ensuring that all objectives at all levels have clear time constraints. o This way the long-term growth of Pinewood is more likely to be achieved. p

e 12/12 marks awarded a The student gives a definition of corporate objectives for 1 AO1 mark. b, c and d The student gives a reason why corporate objectives are important using the extracts and showing good application and good analysis for 2 AO2 marks and 2 AO3 marks. e, f and g The student gives a good evaluation of corporate objectives with good context and a good understanding of how corporate objectives can be ineffective, gaining 1 AO1 mark and 2 AO4 marks. h, i and j The student gives a further benefit of corporate objectives with excellent analysis and context for 2 AO3 marks. k and l The student evaluates why corporate objectives may be unimportant to Pinewood with excellent evaluation for 1 AO4 mark. m, n, o and p The student gives a reasoned conclusion with a recommendation of how to reduce the risks of using corporate objectives in context for 1 AO4 mark.

Student A makes good use of the extract and gives analysis and evaluation of the business concept, but their answer is confused in places and lacks detail. The conclusion is a trap some students fall into, that of simply repeating what they have previously stated in their answer, therefore gaining few or no extra marks. However, it is still a reasonably good response (B grade).

Student B develops a small number of points in detail, which is another approach which can score highly. Excellent use is made of evidence from the extracts and a clear judgement is given related to the MOPS elements. The long-term effect of corporate culture is also considered (A* grade).

SWOT and Porter's five forces analysis

Pinewood Studios is considering how to manage its objective of doubling in size and two options are being considered using SWOT or Porter's five forces analysis.

Analyse and evaluate these two options and recommend which is the most suitable for a business such as Pinewood Studios. (14 marks)

e The 'analyse' and 'evaluate' command words mean you need to review the pros and cons of the two options in detail and of the business term using material from the extracts. You will need to weigh up strengths and weaknesses to support a specific judgement forming a recommendation and conclusion. The extracts should be used to provide application.

AO1: is for giving a reason, a definition or some knowledge of a SWOT or five forces analysis, showing excellent understanding of these business terms. This is worth up to 3 marks.

AO2: for good application of how SWOT and five forces analysis can apply to Pinewood achieving growth. You will need to clearly reference the extracts to support your argument. This is worth up to 3 marks.

AO3: for giving good analysis of how the identified issues are important for the success of Pinewood Studios. This is worth up to 3 marks.

AO4: for giving an excellent evaluation of the relevant factors affecting the merits of SWOT and five forces analysis, assessed in the context of Pinewood Studios. You should make a supported judgement about the business terms in the context of the question, and possibly provide a recommendation and conclusion about the best approach for Pinewood Studios. This is worth up to 5 marks.

Student A

SWOT stands for internal strengths and weaknesses, and external opportunities and threats. a A benefit of SWOT analysis to Pinewood is that it allows the business to look at any external threats to its £200 million expansion project. b Pinewood can also look at the opportunities it can take advantage of by going through this expansion. c For example, more film-makers will want to use the facilities when they are built so Pinewood can take advantage of this demand. d By using SWOT analysis, it can predict how much profit it can make from the expansion. e

However, SWOT analysis may not identify threats from other studios to the expansion. f As a consequence, the project might fail and the business might lose any profits it expected from the £200 million expansion. g

Five forces analysis looks at the threat of new entrants to the film-studio market. h For example, as the expansion project is going to take 15 years, there may be new studios being built that can offer the same facilities at lower cost. i As making films is an expensive process, five forces analysis would state that the bargaining power of buyers would be high and they may decide not to use the new studios built by Pinewood and go to other studios. j As a consequence, five forces analysis would show that there would be a high risk of the expansion project failing and Pinewood losing a lot of money. k

Five forces analysis would be a better option for Pinewood to use as it can identify potential competitors that could pose a risk to the business and then Pinewood could make sure it takes steps to ensure these competitors do not affect its expansion plans. l

ⓔ 9/14 marks awarded ⓐ The student gives a definition of SWOT for 1 AO1 mark. ⓑ The student gives evidence of the relevance of SWOT analysis to the question gaining 1 AO1 mark and 1 AO2 mark. ⓒ and ⓓ The student develops a benefit SWOT analysis to Pinewood with evidence, though it makes assumptions so only gains 1 AO2 mark and 1 AO3 mark. ⓔ The student makes a sweeping assumption of a benefit of SWOT which is undeveloped and gains no marks. ⓕ and ⓖ The student attempts to evaluate SWOT using evidence but as this is not developed and is based on assumptions, it only gains 1 AO4 mark. ⓗ and ⓘ The student attempts to give a benefit of five forces analysis with evidence gaining 1 AO2 mark and 1 AO3 mark. ⓙ and ⓚ The student attempts to make a further analytical point about five forces analysis but as it is based on assumptions, it only gains 1 AO1 mark. ⓛ The student attempts a recommendation but it is superficial and makes no comparisons with SWOT analysis, so gains no marks.

Student B

Both SWOT and five forces analysis aim to give Pinewood a strategic and tactical framework with which to consider the environment the business operates in so that the business can make a plan to manage any potential issues that may affect its objective of doubling in size. ⓐ SWOT analysis is a method for analysing a business, its resources and its environment and stands for internal strengths and weaknesses and external opportunities and threats. ⓑ For example, a key internal strength of Pinewood may be its long track record of success in managing large film productions such as the James Bond films together with a small group of highly skilled technicians. ⓒ. This means that US productions are more likely to use Pinewood's facilities and as the size of this type of work is very large at £1.2 billion, SWOT would seem to indicate that as long as this high level of skill is maintained then the objective of doubling in size is achievable. ⓓ A key threat to Pinewood are the US studios and in the longer term, new Chinese studios such as those being built by the Wanda Group. ⓔ SWOT analysis allows Pinewood to identify these threats and then develop strategies to convert them into strengths. ⓕ For example, the doubling in size of Pinewood and the fact that it has more highly skilled technicians than the Chinese studios would act as a barrier to such competitors being able to derail the expansion by taking away customers. ⓖ

However, SWOT does tend to oversimplify the analysis of threats and opportunities. ⓗ For example, there may be potential competitors who are not yet known to Pinewood who could take valuable customers away from its facilities and mean the doubling in growth could be jeopardised. ⓘ

Porter's five forces analysis is a framework for analysing the nature of competition within an industry or market. It specifically considers the threat of new entrants to a market, the bargaining power of suppliers and customers, the threat of substitute products and the degree of competitive rivalry. ⓙ In some ways, five forces analysis allows Pinewood to complete the same analysis of the threats to its £200 million expansion project as SWOT analysis does. ⓚ For example, it would encourage Pinewood to consider in detail the threat to its expansion from Chinese and US competitors just as SWOT analysis would. ⓛ

However, five forces analysis can be seen as a better tool for Pinewood to use because it provides a more detailed framework to use to analyse the film studio market. m Threats from new entrants may show that there are only a few businesses dominating the market, such as Pinewood, so five forces analysis may describe the rivalry between the businesses as low. n Also barriers to entry — the ability of competitors to enter a market — could be considered as very high for this industry, based on the large amount of money needed to set up a studio and the technical barriers to entry achieved by Pinewood having a unique and highly skilled workforce. o Therefore, five forces allows Pinewood to make a more detailed analysis and highlights the possible decisions of potential competitors that could jeopardise its expansion, which SWOT analysis may not have shown. p However, five forces analysis assumes market forces do not change and clearly the film industry is changing, for example, the more state-of-the-art skills that are needed in making a film. q Five forces would also not consider the clearly large positive effect on the film industry that tax incentives have, encouraging Hollywood production companies to choose to use Pinewood's studios. r SWOT analysis could consider both these issues in its framework so it may be considered as a less risky analysis tool. s

Using just SWOT or Porter's five forces analysis runs the risk of missing out on the identification, analysis and creation of a wide-ranging corporate strategy for dealing with an expansion project over 15 years, and this is something that investors will be concerned about. t Pinewood needs to use a wide range of decision-making tools with SWOT and five forces analysis being just two of the evidence-based decision-making tools needed to ensure risks of growth are kept to a minimum. u Investors are likely to put as much trust into the subjective decision-making skills and intuition of Chief Executive Dunleavy as he has a long track record of success with Pinewood. v All these tools need to be used over the period of 15 years to ensure that the objective of doubling growth is successful. w

e 14/14 marks awarded a The student gives the purpose of SWOT and five forces analysis and a benefit for 1 AO1 mark. b The student then gives a definition of SWOT, gaining a further 1 AO1 mark. c and d The student develops a benefit of SWOT analysis in detail with evidence, gaining 1 AO2 mark and 1 AO3 mark. e The student shows how SWOT analysis can help to identify a potential threat in the context of Pinewood for 1 AO2 mark and 1 AO3 mark. f and g The student gives a benefit of SWOT analysis in being able to counter a potential threat, using evidence from the extracts and gaining 1 AO3 mark. h and i The student evaluates SWOT analysis though there is little development so this only gains 1 AO4 mark. j, k and l The student gives a definition of five forces analysis and a benefit with evidence while also comparing it with SWOT analysis, gaining 1 AO1 mark. m, n and o The student then gives a developed example of how five forces analysis can be of more benefit to Pinewood than SWOT analysis in helping to ensure the objective of doubling growth with detailed use of evidence, gaining 1 AO3 mark. p, q and r The comparison of SWOT and fives forces analysis continues with good use of evidence from the extracts gaining 1 AO4 mark. s The student evaluates SWOT analysis against five forces analysis briefly but there is little development so no further credit is gained. t The student reaches a conclusion that looks at the wider

implications of the two possible approaches to the expansion, gaining 1 AO4 mark.
🅤, 🅥 and 🅦 The student makes a clear recommendation and briefly outlines how this
could be implemented looking at the MOPs elements and using a wider knowledge
of the influences on business decisions with evidence, gaining 2 AO4 marks.

Student A's answer is lacking in detail, and the ideas could have been developed
more clearly. Some evidence is used to support the points made, but the answer
jumps from one point to another. The student may have benefited from writing
a brief plan before writing their answer, which is a good strategy for longer
questions. Overall, a C grade.

Student B makes excellent use of a wide range of business concepts and includes
a detailed knowledge of both SWOT and five forces analysis, comparing the
strengths and weaknesses of both in the context of Pinewood's objective of
doubling in size. A problem for this type of question is that trying to show the
benefits of each approach in great detail risks the student running out of time
and not completing the answer. This student has taken a better approach and
has picked up on only one or two key examples of SWOT and five forces analysis.
They could have developed this further but the answer is still excellent, and
the recommendation and implementation displays an understanding of related
business concepts to gain full marks (A* grade).

1 One reason is that by analysing the sales for each day, the shop can predict which day has the greatest demand for its cakes. The shop could then order more stock for this day to encourage further sales.

2 Price elasticity of demand measures the responsiveness of demand after a change in price. The formula is:

$$PED = \frac{\text{percentage change in quantity demanded}}{\text{percentage change in price}}$$

3 An advantage is that demand will not reduce significantly if the price of the good goes up. This applies to many luxury brands such as Gucci handbags or Apple iPhones. However, very few goods are totally inelastic so there is a point at which customers will decide not to buy an iPhone, if it is felt it is just too expensive. For example, would you pay £1,000 for an iPhone X?

4 Income elasticity of demand measures the responsiveness of demand after a change in customer income. The formula is:

$$YED = \frac{\text{percentage change in quantity demanded}}{\text{percentage change in income}}$$

5 When customer incomes are increasing. This is because Aldi's products are at the discount end of supermarket goods and are therefore likely to be classed as inferior goods.

6 The sales forecast should be reduced at a time of an economic recession because customers may no longer have the disposable income to cover such luxury purchases.

7 One situation would be population demographics as they change relatively slowly over time.

8 Having switched to running an online website only, the *Independent* now has no costs associated with printing and distributing a physical newspaper.

9 One type of business is a seller of fast food such as Subway as the food is a perishable product that needs to be made and sold quickly.

10 One example is a luxury car dealership as there are relatively few buyers of expensive cars.

11 It is likely to be a benefit for a business with high gearing as the business will have a lot of debt, which incurs interest. The lower the interest rate, the lower the costs it will incur on its debt.

12 Decisions to invest are based on many factors, not just the previous performance of a business. As the new venture has no accounts, other documents such as business plans and sales and cash-flow forecasts will need to be used instead. Investors will also be interested in the sales figures of the Land Rover Defender, why it ceased being built and the potential customer demand now.

13 One example is IKEA. It is currently on target to operate 324 wind turbines and 700,000 solar panels so that by 2020, the business will generate all its own power. IKEA's goal in 2017 is that 50% of its wood products come from sustainable forests.

14 One reason is that it can create a link between the vision of the business and how essential its staff are in achieving the vision. An example is IKEA's mission statement: 'Our vision is to create a better everyday life for many people'. This may motivate staff as they can translate it into the customer service they offer as they may aspire to this goal personally.

15 One reason is that the business, team or member of staff may not understand exactly what the objective wants them to achieve, so even with great effort the outcome may not be what was wanted in the first place.

16 Getting an independent person such as a management consultant to perform the SWOT analysis could avoid the pitfall of not being critical enough of the business in terms of its weaknesses and external threats. It can also free up managers' time, especially in a dynamic market where the time to consider every decision is at a premium and competitive advantage may be lost by focusing too much on a SWOT analysis.

17 As China does not allow free movement of information and closely controls inward investment, it will be difficult to gather the type of market research needed to look at existing competitors, for example business size. Also in China, the state strictly controls who can enter local markets and often businesses have to partner with local companies to gain access. Non-market forces such as these are not considered in the five forces framework.

18 The best approach would be market penetration as this would maintain or increase the product's market share in the existing market.

19 A business in a dynamic market may need to react quickly to rapid changes by gaining the skills it needs from another business in order to gain competitive advantage, so external growth would be more appropriate.

20 If the management team have resisted the takeover, they will either leave the new business or be forced to leave. This may result in a loss of management capability for the business, especially if the managers had specialist skills and knowledge.

21 Microsoft was already working closely with Nokia and as the two businesses had different but complementary capabilities — hardware and software manufacture — this led to a best strategic fit in terms of technology and increased competitiveness.

22 The US as well as the UK government have the power to stop a merger if they feel it is not in the customers' best interests. This is particularly the case here as the merger of Coca-Cola and PepsiCo would result in a powerful monopoly and the US government would be worried that this would lead to higher prices and little incentive for the new business to innovate or lower its costs. Coca-Cola and PepsiCo would probably argue that, with increased global competition, a monopoly would benefit customers through increasing economies of scale, leading to lower costs and lower prices.

23 Apple may have created its new headquarters in order to rationalise its operations by housing all its 12,000 staff in one building that is run entirely on renewable energy and allowing for decision making and innovation to take place on one site.

24 Decision trees work well when there are only a few options to consider but are difficult to use when there are many potential options, which is probably the case for an £18 billion nuclear power station. IT could make decision trees more effective as the data can be entered in a simplified way and a computer can do all the calculations.

25 To make critical path analysis more effective a business should also consider the cost and/or quality of each task as both potentially have an effect on the time taken.

26 Payback answers the simple question 'When do I get my money back?'

27 Payback acts as a reality check because it can be viewed as the least testing form of investment appraisal, so if an investment does not do well with this test, then it is unlikely that more stringent calculations will show a good financial return.

28 Environmentally friendly projects are difficult to quantify in terms of money and are only likely to see financial rewards in the medium to long term, when forecasting runs the risk of being much more inaccurate.

29 The level of contribution per unit would go up, meaning the business would have a greater amount available to help cover its fixed costs.

Index